AINS 22 Course Guide

Personal Insurance
3rd Edition

The Institutes
720 Providence Road, Suite 100
Malvern, Pennsylvania 19355-3433

3rd Edition • 2nd Printing • May 2018

ISBN: 978-0-89463-968-5

Contents

Study Materials Available for AINS 22

Personal Insurance, 3rd ed., 2017, AICPCU.

The CPCU Handbook of Insurance Policies, AICPCU.

AINS 22 *Course Guide*, 3rd ed., 2017, AICPCU (includes access code for SMART Online Practice Exams).

AINS 22 SMART Study Aids—Review Notes and Flash Cards, 3rd ed.

Student Resources

Catalog A complete listing of our offerings can be found in The Institutes' professional development catalog, including information about:

- Current programs and courses
- Current textbooks, course guides, SMART Study Aids, and online offerings
- Program completion requirements
- Exam registration

To obtain a copy of the catalog, visit our website at TheInstitutes.org or contact Customer Success at (800) 644-2101.

How to Prepare for Institutes Exams This free handbook is designed to help you by:

- Giving you ideas on how to use textbooks and course guides as effective learning tools
- Providing steps for answering exam questions effectively
- Recommending exam-day strategies

The handbook is printable from the Student Services Center on The Institutes' website at TheInstitutes.org or available by calling Customer Success at (800) 644-2101.

Educational Counseling Services To ensure that you take courses matching both your needs and your skills, you can obtain free counseling from The Institutes by:

- Emailing your questions to Advising@TheInstitutes.org
- Calling an Institutes counselor directly at (610) 644-2100, ext. 7601
- Obtaining and completing a self-inventory form, available on our website at TheInstitutes.org or by contacting Customer Success at (800) 644-2101

Exam Registration Information As you proceed with your studies, be sure to arrange for your exam.

- Visit our website at TheInstitutes.org/forms to access and print the Registration Booklet, which contains information and forms needed to register for your exam.
- Plan to register with The Institutes well in advance of your exam.

How to Contact The Institutes For more information on any of these publications and services:

- Visit our website at TheInstitutes.org
- Call us at (800) 644-2101 or (610) 644-2100 outside the U.S.
- Email us at CustomerSuccess@TheInstitutes.org
- Fax us at (610) 640-9576
- Write to us at The Institutes, Customer Service, 720 Providence Road, Suite 100, Malvern, PA 19355-3433

Using This Course Guide

This course guide will help you learn the course content and prepare for the exam.

Each assignment in this course guide typically includes the following components:

Educational Objectives These are the most important study tools in the course guide. Because all of the questions on the exam are based on the Educational Objectives, the best way to study for the exam is to focus on these objectives.

Each Educational Objective typically begins with one of the following action words, which indicate the level of understanding required for the exam:

Analyze—Determine the nature and the relationship of the parts.

Apply—Put to use for a practical purpose.

Associate—Bring together into relationship.

Calculate—Determine numeric values by mathematical process.

Classify—Arrange or organize according to class or category.

Compare—Show similarities and differences.

Contrast—Show only differences.

Define—Give a clear, concise meaning.

Describe—Represent or give an account.

Determine—Settle or decide.

Evaluate—Determine the value or merit.

Explain—Relate the importance or application.

Identify or list—Name or make a list.

Illustrate—Give an example.

Justify—Show to be right or reasonable.

Paraphrase—Restate in your own words.

Recommend—Suggest or endorse something to be used.

Summarize—Concisely state the main points.

Outline The outline lists the topics in the assignment. Read the outline before the required reading to become familiar with the assignment content and the relationships of topics.

Key Words and Phrases These words and phrases are fundamental to understanding the assignment and have a common meaning for those working in insurance. After completing the required reading, test your understanding of the assignment's Key Words and Phrases by writing their definitions.

Review Questions The review questions test your understanding of what you have read. Review the Educational Objectives and required reading, then answer the questions to the best of your ability. When you are finished, check the answers at the end of the assignment to evaluate your comprehension.

Application Questions These questions continue to test your knowledge of the required reading by applying what you've studied to "hypothetical" real-life situations. Again, check the suggested answers at the end of the assignment to review your progress.

Sample Exam Your course guide includes a sample exam (located at the back) or a code for accessing SMART Online Practice Exams (which appears on the inside of the cover). Use the option available for the course you're taking to become familiar with the test format. SMART Online Practice Exams are as close as you can get to experiencing an actual exam before taking one.

More Study Aids

The Institutes also produce supplemental study tools, called SMART Study Aids, for many of our courses. When SMART Study Aids are available for a course, they are listed on page iii of the course guide. SMART Study Aids include Review Notes and Flash Cards and are excellent tools to help you learn and retain the information in each assignment.

A

▶▶

Direct Your Learning

Personal Insurance Overview

Educational Objectives

After learning the content of this assignment, you should be able to:

1. Summarize the three elements of loss exposures.

2. Describe the property loss exposures that individuals and families might face in terms of each of the following:

   - The assets exposed to loss

   - The causes of loss

   - The financial consequences of loss

3. Describe the liability loss exposures that individuals and families might face in terms of each of the following:

   - The assets exposed to loss

   - The causes of loss

   - The financial consequences of loss

4. Describe the personal financial planning loss exposures that individuals and families might face in terms of each of the following:

   - The assets exposed to loss

   - The causes of loss

   - The financial consequences of loss

5. Demonstrate how the six steps of the risk management process can guide individuals and families in their risk management decisions.

6. Describe how risk control and risk financing techniques are used by individuals and families.

7. Explain how personal insurance is used as a risk management technique.

1

8. Summarize the contents of the six common categories of policy provisions of a property-casualty insurance policy.

9. Describe the primary methods of insurance policy analysis.

Outline

▶ **Elements of Loss Exposures**
   A. Asset Exposed to Loss
   B. Cause of Loss
   C. Financial Consequence of Loss
▶ **Property Loss Exposures**
   A. Assets Exposed to Loss
      1. Real Property
      2. Personal Property
   B. Causes of Loss
   C. Financial Consequences of Loss
▶ **Liability Loss Exposures**
   A. Assets Exposed to Loss
   B. Causes of Loss
      1. Tort Liability
      2. Contractual Liability
      3. Statutory Liability
   C. Financial Consequences of Loss
▶ **Personal Financial Planning Loss Exposures**
   A. Retirement Loss Exposures
   B. Premature Death Loss Exposures
   C. Health and Disability Loss Exposures
   D. Unemployment
▶ **Risk Management Process**
   A. Step 1: Identifying Loss Exposures
   B. Step 2: Analyzing Loss Exposures
   C. Step 3: Examining the Feasibility of Risk Management Techniques
   D. Step 4: Selecting the Appropriate Risk Management Techniques
   E. Step 5: Implementing the Selected Risk Management Techniques
   F. Step 6: Monitoring Results and Revising the Risk Management Program
▶ **Risk Management Techniques**
   A. Risk Control Techniques
      1. Avoidance
      2. Loss Prevention
      3. Loss Reduction

      4. Separation
      5. Duplication
      6. Diversification
   B. Risk Financing Techniques
      1. Retention
      2. Transfer
▶ **Insurance as a Risk Financing Technique**
   A. Property and Liability Loss Exposures
   B. Retirement Loss Exposures
   C. Premature Death Loss Exposures
   D. Health and Disability Loss Exposures
   E. Unemployment Loss Exposures
▶ **Common Policy Provisions**
   A. Declarations
   B. Definitions
   C. Insuring Agreements
   D. Conditions
   E. Exclusions
   F. Miscellaneous Provisions
▶ **Policy Analysis**
   A. Pre-Loss Policy Analysis
   B. Post-Loss Policy Analysis

s.m.a.r.t.®
tips

Don't spend time on material you have already mastered. The SMART Review Notes are organized by the Educational Objectives found in each assignment to help you track your study.

For each assignment, you should define or describe each of the Key Words and Phrases and answer each of the Review and Application Questions.

Educational Objective 1
Summarize the three elements of loss exposures.

Key Words and Phrases

Loss exposure

Cause of loss (peril)

Review Questions

1-1. What is an asset exposed to loss?

1-2. What is a cause of loss?

1-3. The financial consequences of loss are dependent on what factors?

Application Question

1-4. Joe has just purchased a new home. Assess whether all the necessary elements of a loss exposure are present.

Educational Objective 2

Describe the property loss exposures that individuals and families might face in terms of each of the following:

- **The assets exposed to loss**
- **The causes of loss**
- **The financial consequences of loss**

Key Words and Phrases

Property loss exposure

Real property (realty)

Personal property

Review Questions

2-1. What is a property loss exposure?

2-2. Individuals and families may own assets that are exposed to loss. Assets are any items of property that have value.

    a.   What are two types of property that individuals and families own that may be exposed to loss?

    b.   For your answers to (a), provide an example for each.

2-3. Name some causes of loss that might damage or destroy a dwelling.

2-4. What are three financial consequences of loss?

Application Question

2-5. Virtually all individuals and families have property loss exposures. Assume a family owns a fully furnished home that includes a yard, storage shed, and several fruit trees.

    a. What are the assets exposed to loss that the family might have as a consequence of home ownership?

    b. What are the causes of loss the family might face as a consequence of home ownership?

    c. What are the financial consequences of loss the family might face arising from home ownership?

Educational Objective 3

Describe the liability loss exposures that individuals and families might face in terms of each of the following:

- **The assets exposed to loss**
- **The causes of loss**
- **The financial consequences of loss**

Key Words and Phrases

Liability loss exposure

Damages

General damages

Special damages

Punitive damages (exemplary damages)

Civil law

Tort

Negligence

Review Questions

3-1. Identify the assets exposed to loss in a liability loss exposure.

3-2. Identify the cause of loss associated with a liability loss exposure.

3-3. Describe the financial consequences of a liability loss exposure.

3-4. Identify the four elements of negligence.

3-5. Identify four examples of intentional torts.

Application Question

3-6. Sean has a disagreement with his neighbor, John, and physically harms him, causing John to be admitted to the hospital. John subsequently files a lawsuit against Sean.

   a.   Which of Sean's assets are exposed to loss?

   b.   What is the cause of Sean's loss?

   c.   What are the potential financial consequences for Sean?

Educational Objective 4

Describe the personal financial planning loss exposures that individuals and families might face in terms of each of the following:

- **The assets exposed to loss**
- **The causes of loss**
- **The financial consequences of loss**

Key Words and Phrases

Personal financial planning loss exposures

Temporary partial disability (TPD)

Temporary total disability (TTD)

Permanent partial disability (PPD)

Permanent total disability (PTD)

Review Questions

4-1. Identify the assets exposed to loss when an individual retires.

4-2. Describe the causes of loss associated with health and disability loss exposures.

4-3. Identify the four types of disability classifications.

Application Question

4-4. Assume Anton, a husband and father, dies prematurely.

    a.   What are the assets exposed to loss as a result of his death?

    b.   What is the financial cause of loss?

Educational Objective 5

Demonstrate how the six steps of the risk management process can guide individuals and families in their risk management decisions.

Key Words and Phrases

Risk management process

Risk control

Risk financing

Review Questions

5-1. List the six steps of the risk management process.

5-2. Describe the loss characteristics that individuals and families may use to analyze their loss exposures.

5-3. Describe examples of measures that individuals and families might use to implement the selected risk management techniques.

Application Question

5-4. A family plans to analyze its automobile loss exposures. The mother and father each drive an older-model car. Their three daughters live with them and regularly use their cars in the evenings. Over the last three years, the family has been involved in four minor auto accidents. How might the family use the four dimensions of a loss exposure to analyze its automobile loss exposures?

Educational Objective 6

Describe how risk control and risk financing techniques are used by individuals and families.

Key Words and Phrases

Avoidance

Loss prevention

Loss reduction

Separation

Duplication

Diversification

Retention

Insurance

Transfer

Review Questions

6-1. Identify the risk control techniques used by individuals and families.

6-2. Identify the risk financing techniques used by individuals and families.

6-3. Describe two noninsurance risk transfer techniques.

6-4. Compare loss prevention to loss reduction.

6-5. Contrast planned retention with unplanned retention.

Application Question

6-6. For each of these sets of frequency-severity characteristics, explain whether you would retain or transfer a personal loss exposure with those characteristics:

a. Low severity and low frequency

b.   High severity and low frequency

c.   Low severity and high frequency

d.   Medium severity and medium frequency

Educational Objective 7
Explain how personal insurance is used as a risk management technique.

Key Word or Phrase

Workers compensation

Review Questions

7-1. Identify the risk financing techniques individuals and families use to manage their loss exposures.

7-2. Identify the three layers of personal insurance.

7-3. Contrast the sources of property and liability loss exposures.

7-4. Identify examples of retirement loss exposures.

7-5. Describe how individuals and families can mitigate the financial consequences of retirement loss exposures.

7-6. Identify an example of a premature death loss exposure.

7-7. Contrast the needs-based approach and the human life value approach used to determine the amount of insurance that an individual or a family should purchase.

7-8. Why may health and disability insurance be more important to an individual or a family than life insurance?

7-9. Under what circumstances would a state extend the period over which unemployed individuals can receive benefits?

Application Question

7-10. Jerry and Linda are forty-five and forty-two years of age, respectively. They have three children, ages eighteen, fifteen, and twelve. Jerry is employed full-time. Identify the types of insurance that the family should consider to manage the risks it faces.

Educational Objective 8

Summarize the contents of the six common categories of policy provisions of a property-casualty insurance policy.

Key Words and Phrases

Policy provision

Declarations page (declarations, or dec.)

Endorsement

Definitions

Insuring agreement

Policy condition

Exclusion

Review Questions

8-1. Summarize the contents of a property-casualty insurance policy's declarations.

8-2. Describe the interpretation rules a policy applies to undefined words and phrases.

8-3. Summarize the contents of a property-casualty insurance policy's insuring agreement.

Application Question

8-4. Paul, a policy analyst, needs to know the effect on coverage of each of the insurance policy provision categories. Paul's boss, Rachel, asks you to create a chart to assist Paul in learning the effect of each of the policy provision categories. What would you include in the chart to note the effect on coverage of each of the policy provision categories?

Educational Objective 9

Describe the primary methods of insurance policy analysis.

Review Questions

9-1. Describe the sources of information insureds may use to generate scenarios for pre-loss policy analysis.

9-2. Describe a limitation of scenario analysis.

9-3. Describe the primary method of post-loss policy analysis.

Application Question

9-4. A family's home is destroyed by a fire. Explain how a claims adjuster for the home's insurer could determine whether the loss was covered by the family's homeowners policy.

Answers to Assignment 1 Questions

NOTE: These answers are provided to give students a basic understanding of acceptable types of responses. They often are not the only valid answers and are not intended to provide an exhaustive response to the questions.

Educational Objective 1

1-1. An asset exposed to loss can be any item with value that is exposed to a possible reduction in value due to loss.

1-2. A cause of loss (or peril) is the means by which an asset can be reduced in value.

1-3. The financial consequences of loss are dependent on these factors:

- Type of asset exposed to loss

- Cause of loss

- Severity of loss

1-4. All the elements of a loss exposure are present for Joe:

- Asset exposed to loss—Joe's new home.

- Cause of loss—The possibility that a loss (a reduction in value to the asset) could occur to the new home.

- Financial consequences—If a loss occurs, it generates financial consequences for Joe.

Educational Objective 2

2-1. A property loss exposure is any condition or situation that presents the possibility of a property loss.

2-2. These answers address questions regarding the assets owned by individuals and families:

a. Two types of property that individuals and families own that may be exposed to loss are (1) real property and (2) personal property.

b. (1) Examples of real property that may be exposed to loss can include a home, foundations, underground pipes, sheds attached to the land, or anything growing on the land, including trees. (Other real property examples are acceptable.)

(2) Examples of personal property that may be exposed to loss can include furniture; televisions; electronic equipment, including computers; and additional household personal property, such as appliances, dishes, carpets, sports equipment, clothing, tools, books, jewelry, cameras, and digital recording devices. Other examples of personal property that may be exposed to loss can include autos, boats, and intangible property. (Other personal property examples are acceptable.)

2-3. Causes of loss (or perils) that can damage or destroy real property, such as a dwelling, include fire, lightning, earthquake, or wind. (Other real property/dwelling cause of loss examples are acceptable.)

2-4. Financial consequences of loss can include one or more of these outcomes:

- Reduction in value of property—the difference between the value of the property before the loss (pre-loss value) and after the loss (post-loss value).

- Increased expenses—expenses in addition to normal living expenses that are necessary because of the loss.

- Lost income—loss of income that results if property is damaged.

2-5. These answers address questions regarding the property loss exposures of individuals and families:

a. Assets exposed to loss include real property and personal property. Real property can include the family's home, foundation, any underground pipes, the storage shed, the land, and the fruit trees. Personal property is all property other than real property, including all the furnishings (or contents) of the home. Such household furnishings for the family might include furniture, carpets, electronics, dishware, clothing, appliances, and numerous other items. (Other real property and personal property examples are acceptable).

b. Causes of loss damage or destroy both real and personal property. As a consequence of home ownership, the family might face such causes of loss affecting their dwelling and furnishings as fire, lightning, earthquake, or wind. (Other causes of loss examples are acceptable).

c. Financial consequences of loss the family might face arising from home ownership include one or more of these outcomes:

- Reduction in value to the home and furnishings—If a loss occurs, the value of the home and its contents may be less after the loss than it was worth before the loss.

- Increased expenses—If a loss occurs to the home and its furnishings, the family may face increased living expenses (such as the cost of hotel room rental) in addition to normal living expenses.

- Lost income—If a loss occurs, in some instances, the family may suffer loss of income as a result of the property damage.

Educational Objective 3

3-1. The assets exposed to loss in a liability loss exposure are money or other financial assets.

3-2. The cause of loss associated with a liability loss exposure is the claim of liability or the filing of a lawsuit.

3-3. The financial consequences of a liability loss exposure are that an individual or a family may lose money or other financial assets. For example, they may have to pay to investigate and defend against the liability claim. Also, a court may award monetary damages if the defense of the claim is not successful or if the claim is settled out of court.

3-4. These are the four elements of negligence:

- A duty to act.

- A breach of that duty.

- An injury or damage occurs.

- The breach of duty is a direct cause of the injury or damage in an unbroken chain of events.

3-5. These are examples of intentional torts:

- Libel

- Slander

- Assault

- Battery

- Trespass

- Nuisance

3-6. These answers address questions regarding John's lawsuit against Sean.

a. The assets exposed to loss are Sean's money and other financial assets.

b. The cause of loss for Sean is the lawsuit filed by John.

c. Sean may need to pay general, special, and punitive damages as a result of the liability suit.

Educational Objective 4

4-1. The assets exposed to loss when an individual retires are the individual's regular employment income and the related benefits, such as health insurance.

4-2. The causes of loss associated with health and disability loss exposures are chronic illness and/or physical or mental disability.

4-3. These are the four types of disability classifications:

- Temporary partial disability

- Temporary total disability

- Permanent partial disability

- Permanent total disability

4-4. These answers address questions regarding Anton's premature death.

a. Assets exposed to loss as the result of Anton's premature death include the expected income on which his wife and family rely.

b. The financial cause of loss is the loss of the income that Anton could have earned had he remained alive. If replacement income from his life insurance, other financial assets, and Social Security does not meet his family's needs, it will likely experience considerable financial hardship.

Educational Objective 5

5-1. These are the six steps of the risk management process:

    a. Identify loss exposures

    b. Analyze loss exposures

    c. Examine the feasibility of risk management techniques

    d. Select the appropriate risk management techniques

    e. Implement the selected risk management techniques

    f. Monitor results and revise the risk management program

5-2. The loss characteristics that individuals and families may use to analyze their loss exposures are loss frequency, loss severity, total dollar losses, and timing of losses.

5-3. These are examples of measures individuals and families may use to implement selected risk management techniques:

- Purchasing loss reduction devices

- Contracting for loss prevention services

- Implementing loss control programs

- Obtaining expert advice on how to deal with challenging loss exposures

- Obtaining insurance policies for loss exposures they are not willing to retain

- Creating a list of possessions that may be subject to loss

5-4. The family might analyze its automobile loss exposures in this manner:

- First, it analyzes loss frequency. Four accidents over the last three years are a concern.

- Next, it analyzes loss severity. All four accidents were minor. Perhaps the family would consider maintaining higher collision deductibles on the two older-model cars. The family might retain the cost of minor accidents to avoid increased insurance premiums.

- It would then analyze total dollar losses. The four accidents were minor. However, the family should maintain high liability limits in case any of its members are subsequently involved in a serious auto accident. Even if one of the older cars has to be replaced instead of repaired, the cost of a new vehicle could be covered by family savings.

- Finally, it would analyze the timing of the accidents. Damage from the four accidents was easily repaired. However, the family still should account for the possibility of a future severe liability claim that may cost millions of dollars.

Educational Objective 6

6-1. The risk control techniques individuals and families use include these:

- Avoidance

- Loss prevention

- Loss reduction

- Separation

- Duplication

- Diversification

6-2. The risk financing techniques individuals and families use include these:

- Retention

- Transfer

6-3. A hold-harmless agreement is a noninsurance risk transfer in which one party assumes the legal liability of another party to the contract, such as in an apartment lease. Hedging is another noninsurance risk transfer technique whereby one asset (money) is paid to offset the risk associated with another asset.

6-4. Loss prevention is a risk control technique that reduces the frequency of a particular loss, while loss reduction is a risk control technique that reduces the severity of a particular loss.

6-5. Planned retention is a deliberate assumption of loss that has been identified and analyzed. Unplanned retention is the inadvertent, unplanned assumption of a loss exposure that has not been identified or accurately analyzed.

6-6. These answers address questions regarding frequency-severity characteristics:

a. Losses of low severity and low frequency are predictable and are usually of little financial consequence. These types of losses should be retained.

b. Costs of losses of high severity and low frequency are unpredictable, and they present a high risk. These types of losses would likely be transferred before they occur.

c. Losses of low severity and high frequency are predictable. These types of losses should be retained.

d. Loss exposures of medium severity and medium frequency may be retained or transferred, depending on tolerance for risk and the cost of the risk transfer.

Educational Objective 7

7-1. The risk financing techniques individuals and families use to manage their loss exposures are personal insurance, noninsurance transfers, and retention.

7-2. Personal insurance consists of three layers: social programs of insurance, group insurance, and individual insurance.

7-3. Property loss exposures stem from a legal interest in both real and personal property. Liability loss exposures originate from the possibility of being sued or being held responsible for someone else's injury.

7-4. Examples of the assets exposed to loss when an individual retires include regular employment income and the related benefits of employment, such as health insurance.

7-5. Methods individuals and families use to mitigate the financial consequences of retirement loss exposures include maintaining savings plans and pension plans to help them prepare for retirement. Social Security, an example of social insurance, is available for covered workers who are at least sixty-two years old. Other methods individuals and families may use to mitigate the financial consequences of retirement loss exposures include maintaining individual retirement accounts, employer-sponsored group pension plans, 401(k) savings plans, and defined benefit plans.

7-6. An example of a premature death loss exposure is the expected income on which the deceased's family or heirs rely.

7-7. The needs-based approach attempts to estimate a family's future financial needs after considering any Social Security and other applicable benefits that the family would receive after the death of an income provider. The human life value approach attempts to measure the present value of the financial contribution of the wage earner to the family.

7-8. Health and disability insurance may be more important to an individual or family than life insurance because if a person becomes critically ill or disabled, the cost of hospital care, medication, and care giving could become a severe financial burden. The illness or disability may also prevent a spouse from obtaining employment that would help replace the income generated by the ill or disabled spouse.

7-9. A state may extend the period over which unemployed individuals can receive benefits if economic conditions or state unemployment rates warrant the extension.

7-10. The family might consider selecting from among social insurance, group insurance, and private insurance.

Social insurance provides a basic foundation of coverage. If Jerry, currently the only monetary provider for the family, were to die or become disabled, social insurance in the form of Social Security or workers compensation would likely be available to the family.

Group insurance (life insurance and health insurance) is provided by many employers. The family may augment its group coverage with individual insurance.

Individual insurance is insurance available for individuals and families for their homes and automobiles and other property and liability coverages. A liability umbrella can be purchased relatively inexpensively to cover extensive liability exposures, known as well as unknown.

Educational Objective 8

8-1. The policy declarations typically contain this information:

- Policy or policy number
- Policy inception and expiration dates (policy period)
- Name of the insurer
- Name of the insurance agent
- Name of the insured(s)
- Names of additional interests that are covered
- Mailing address of the insured
- Physical address and description of the covered property
- Numbers and edition dates of attached forms and endorsements
- Dollar amounts of applicable policy limits
- Dollar amounts of applicable deductibles
- Premium

8-2. Undefined words and phrases are interpreted according to these rules of policy interpretation:

- Everyday words are given their ordinary meanings.
- Technical words are given their technical meanings.
- Words with an established legal meaning are given their legal meanings.
- Consideration is given to local, cultural, and trade-usage meanings of words.

8-3. The insuring agreement is the promise of coverage the insurer makes to the insured and is essentially what the insured is buying.

8-4. A chart created to note the effect on coverage of each of the policy provision categories may read:

Policy Provision Category	Effect on Coverage
Declarations	Outline who or what is covered and where and when coverage applies
Definitions	May limit or expand coverage based on definitions of terms
Insuring agreements	Outline circumstances under which the insurer agrees to pay
Conditions	Outline steps insured needs to take to enforce policy
Exclusions	Limit insurer's payments based on excluded persons, places, things, or actions
Miscellaneous	Deal with the relationship between the insured and the insurer or establish procedures for implementing the policy

Educational Objective 9

9-1. For insureds, the primary source of information for generating scenarios for pre-loss policy analysis is their past loss experience. If the insured has not experienced a loss that triggered insurance coverage, friends, neighbors, co-workers, and family members can provide information about their experiences with losses and the claim process. The insurance producer and customer service representative are also good sources of information.

9-2. One of the limitations of scenario analysis is that, because the number of possible loss scenarios is theoretically infinite, it is impossible to account for every possibility.

9-3. The primary method of post-loss policy analysis is the DICE (an acronym representing the policy provision categories: declarations, insuring agreements, conditions, and exclusions) method, which is a systematic review of all the categories of property-casualty policy provisions.

9-4. The claims adjuster would follow the steps specified in the DICE decision tree to determine whether the family's homeowners policy covered the loss.

First, he or she would check the declarations to see whether anything there would preclude coverage. If not, he or she would go to the next step.

Second, he or she would see whether anything in the insuring agreement would preclude coverage. If not, he or she would go to the next step.

Third, he or she would check the conditions to see whether anything precluded coverage and, if not, go to the next step.

Fourth, he or she would check the exclusions and all other policy provisions not already analyzed, including the endorsements and miscellaneous provisions, to make sure that nothing would preclude coverage. If not, he or she would determine the amount payable under the policy.

Direct Your Learning

Automobile Insurance and Society

Educational Objectives

After learning the content of this assignment, you should be able to:

1. Evaluate each of the following approaches to compensating automobile accident victims:

   - Tort liability system
   - Financial responsibility laws
   - Compulsory insurance laws
   - Uninsured motorists coverage
   - Underinsured motorists coverage
   - No-fault insurance

2. Describe no-fault automobile laws in terms of each of the following:

   - Types of no-fault laws
   - Benefits required by no-fault laws

3. Explain how high-risk drivers may obtain auto insurance.

4. Describe automobile insurance rate regulation in terms of each of the following:

   - Rating factors
   - Matching price to exposure
   - Competition
   - Other regulatory issues

Outline

▶ **Compensation of Auto Accident Victims**
 A. Tort Liability System
 B. Financial Responsibility Laws
 C. Compulsory Auto Insurance Laws
 D. Uninsured Motorists Coverage
 E. Underinsured Motorists Coverage
 F. No-Fault Automobile Insurance

▶ **No-Fault Automobile Laws**
 A. Types of No-Fault Laws
  1. Modified No-Fault Plans
  2. Add-On Plans
  3. Choice No-Fault Plans
 B. Benefits Required by No-Fault Laws

▶ **Automobile Insurance for High-Risk Drivers**
 A. Voluntary Market Programs
 B. Residual Market Programs
  1. Automobile Insurance Plans
  2. Joint Underwriting Associations (JUAs)
  3. Other Programs

▶ **Automobile Insurance Rate Regulation**
 A. Rating Factors
  1. Primary Rating Factors
  2. Other Rating Factors
  3. Other Discounts and Credits
 B. Matching Price to Exposure
 C. Competition
 D. Other Regulatory Issues
  1. Rising Healthcare Costs
  2. Environmental Issues
  3. Vehicle Modifications

s.m.a.r.t. tips Reduce the number of Key Words and Phrases that you must review. SMART Flash Cards contain the Key Words and Phrases and their definitions, allowing you to set aside those cards that you have mastered.

▶▶

For each assignment, you should define or describe each of the Key Words and Phrases and answer each of the Review and Application Questions.

Educational Objective 1

Evaluate each of the following approaches to compensating automobile accident victims:

- **Tort liability system**
- **Financial responsibility laws**
- **Compulsory insurance laws**
- **Uninsured motorists coverage**
- **Underinsured motorists coverage**
- **No-fault insurance**

Key Words and Phrases

Financial responsibility law

Compulsory auto insurance law

First party

Unsatisfied judgment fund

Uninsured motorists (UM) coverage

Underinsured motorists (UIM) coverage

No-fault automobile insurance

Review Questions

1-1. Briefly describe how the tort liability system compensates injured auto accident victims.

1-2. Describe three circumstances under which a motorist is required to provide proof of financial responsibility to comply with financial responsibility laws.

1-3. Describe the disadvantages of financial responsibility laws.

1-4. Describe an advantage of compulsory insurance laws, as compared to financial responsibility laws.

1-5. Explain how low-cost auto insurance addresses the problem of uninsured drivers.

1-6. Describe the common characteristics of unsatisfied judgment funds.

1-7. Briefly describe how no-fault automobile insurance operates.

1-8. Explain why no-fault auto insurance laws were developed.

Application Question

1-9. Contrast uninsured motorists coverage (UM) with underinsured motorists coverage (UIM).

Educational Objective 2

Describe no-fault automobile laws in terms of each of the following:

- **Types of no-fault laws**
- **Benefits required by no-fault laws**

Key Words and Phrases

No-fault laws

Monetary threshold (dollar threshold)

Verbal threshold

Add-on plan

Choice no-fault plan

Personal injury protection (PIP) coverage

▶▶

Subrogation

Review Questions

2-1. Contrast a pure no-fault system with modified no-fault plans.

2-2. Explain how add-on plans differ from choice no-fault plans.

2-3. Identify four benefits required by no-fault laws.

2-4. Describe what determines the personal injury protection (PIP) coverage benefits that insurers provide.

Application Question

2-5. Tom lives in a modified no-fault state and carries the minimum PIP medical coverage limit of $20,000 set by the plan. Tom's state has a monetary threshold for noneconomic losses of $50,000. He sustains injuries in an auto accident and incurs $30,000 in economic losses. Tom also suffers $15,000 in noneconomic losses.

    a. What amount of economic losses would Tom collect from his own insurer?

    b. What amount of noneconomic losses would Tom collect from his own insurer?

    c. Can Tom sue the at-fault party for economic losses in this case? Explain your answer.

    d. Can Tom sue the at-fault party for noneconomic losses in this case? Explain your answer.

Educational Objective 3
Explain how high-risk drivers may obtain auto insurance.

Key Words and Phrases

Residual market

Safe driver insurance plan (SDIP)

Automobile insurance plan

Joint underwriting association (JUA)

Reinsurance facility

Review Questions

3-1. Identify two types of programs that provide automobile insurance for high-risk drivers.

3-2.   How do the activities of insurers of high-risk drivers in the voluntary market differ from the activities of insurers in the residual market?

3-3.   Under a state automobile insurance plan, how are the high-risk drivers apportioned to the auto insurers in that state?

3-4.   What roles does a state joint underwriting association (JUA) serve with regard to rates, policy forms, and claim settlement for high-risk drivers?

Application Question

3-5.   XYZ Auto Insurance sells insurance in a state that has a reinsurance facility for high-risk drivers. Mary is a high-risk driver who has obtained insurance from XYZ. XYZ, in turn, assigned Mary to the reinsurance facility. Mary subsequently had an auto accident and is responsible for the damage to Bill's auto and for Bill's injuries.

   a.   Does XYZ or the reinsurance facility accept Mary's application and service her policy?

b. Does XYZ or the reinsurance facility handle Bill's liability claim?

c. What organization(s) bears any underwriting losses that result from Bill's liability claim?

Educational Objective 4

Describe automobile insurance rate regulation in terms of each of the following:

- **Rating factors**
- **Matching price to exposure**
- **Competition**
- **Other regulatory issues**

Review Questions

4-1. Explain these automobile insurance rating factors and why insurers use them:

a. Territory

b.   Age

c.   Driver education

d.   Multi-car policy

e.   Credit-based insurance score

4-2.   Describe the homogeneous classes, or rating categories, that insurers often use to help match price to exposure.

4-3. Explain the relationship between competition and regulatory monitoring of insurance rates and how that monitoring is accomplished.

Application Question

4-4. XYZ Insurance has its home office in a state with a population that consists predominantly of people of a particular ethnic origin. XYZ wanted to encourage state residents to buy insurance policies, so it filed rates with the state insurance regulators that extended a flat 70 percent discount to all applicants of the predominant ethnic origin, after considering other rating factors. Explain why the state regulators might not approve these rates based on each of the following rating objectives.

   a.   Rates must be adequate to pay all claims and expenses.

   b.   Rates must not be unfairly discriminatory.

Answers to Assignment 2 Questions

NOTE: These answers are provided to give students a basic understanding of acceptable types of responses. They often are not the only valid answers and are not intended to provide an exhaustive response to the questions.

Educational Objective 1

1-1. If a driver operates an auto in a negligent manner that results in bodily injury to another person or in damage to another's property, the operator can be held legally liable for damages incurred by the injured person. Under the tort liability system, injured auto accident victims must prove that another party was at fault before they can collect damages from that party.

1-2. A motorist is required to provide proof of financial responsibility under these circumstances:

- After an auto accident involving bodily injury or property damage exceeding a certain dollar amount

- After a conviction for certain serious offenses, such as drunk driving or reckless driving, or after losing a driver's license because of repeated violations

- Upon failure to pay a final judgment that results from an auto accident

1-3. These are disadvantages of financial responsibility laws:

- Most financial responsibility requirements become effective only after an accident, a conviction, or a judgment.

- Financial responsibility laws do not guarantee payment to all accident victims. Persons injured by uninsured drivers, hit-and-run drivers, or drivers of stolen cars might not be compensated.

- Injured persons might not be fully indemnified for their injuries even when injured by motorists who can prove financial responsibility. Most financial responsibility laws set minimum financial requirements, which may not fully compensate a victim.

1-4. An advantage of compulsory insurance laws, as compared to financial responsibility laws, is that motorists must provide proof of financial responsibility before an accident occurs. By requiring proof of financial responsibility prior to an accident, compulsory insurance laws go beyond financial responsibility laws by ensuring that accident victims are compensated for their losses.

1-5. Low-cost auto insurance is intended to decrease the number of uninsured drivers by making minimal liability coverage available at a reduced cost. Low-cost insurance programs are intended to provide some level of protection at a reduced cost to assist lower-income drivers in purchasing the insurance coverage required to comply with compulsory auto insurance laws.

1-6. Unsatisfied judgment funds have these characteristics:

- An injured person can receive compensation from the fund after having obtained a judgment against a negligent driver and proving that the judgment cannot be collected.

- The maximum amount paid is generally limited to the state's minimum compulsory insurance requirement. In addition, most funds reduce the amount paid by any amount the injured person has collected from other collateral sources of recovery, such as workers compensation benefits or insurance.

- The negligent driver is not relieved of legal liability when the unsatisfied judgment fund compensates the insured person. The negligent driver's license is revoked until the driver reimburses the fund.

1-7. Under a no-fault system, an injured person does not need to establish fault and prove negligence in order to collect payment for damages. In addition, certain no-fault laws place some restrictions on an injured person's right to sue a negligent driver who causes an accident. In some states, when a claim is below a certain monetary threshold, the injured motorist collects for injuries under his or her own insurance policy.

1-8. No-fault laws were developed to avoid the costly and time-consuming process of determining legal liability for auto accidents under the tort liability system. By eliminating the need to prove fault, no-fault laws allow accident victims to receive benefits much sooner after an accident and, as a result, may allow for a quicker recovery from injuries.

1-9. UM coverage compensates an insured for bodily injury caused by an uninsured motorist, a hit-and-run driver, or a driver whose insurer is insolvent. UIM coverage, on the other hand, provides additional limits of protection to the victim of an auto accident when the negligent driver's insurance limits are insufficient to pay for the damages.

Educational Objective 2

2-1. In a pure no-fault system, injured persons would not need to establish fault or prove negligence to collect payment for damages, but they also would not be able to seek damages through the tort liability system. In contrast, under a modified no-fault plan, injured persons would collect economic losses from their own insurers based on state-mandated PIP benefits, and they can sue at-fault drivers for any economic losses that exceed the no-fault coverage limits.

2-2. An add-on plan allows injured drivers the option of collecting for economic losses through their own insurer, but it places no restrictions on their right to sue a negligent party for damages. In contrast, a choice no-fault plan enables the insured to choose whether to be covered on a modified no-fault basis at the time the policy is purchased or renewed. Under a choice plan, insureds who choose the modified no-fault option have limitations on the right to sue for certain types of auto injuries. Insureds who do not choose the modified no-fault option retain full rights to seek compensation from the negligent party, but they pay a higher premium than those insureds who choose the modified no-fault option.

2-3. Benefits required by no-fault laws include these:

- Medical expenses

- Rehabilitation expenses

- Loss of earnings

- Expenses for essential services

- Funeral expenses

- Survivors' loss benefits

2-4. PIP benefits are determined by state no-fault laws.

2-5. These answers address questions regarding Tom's auto accident:

a. Tom would collect $20,000 in economic losses from his own insurer because his PIP medical coverage is limited to $20,000 and his economic losses ($30,000) exceed the limit.

b. Under modified no-fault laws, insureds cannot collect for noneconomic losses through their PIP coverage, so Tom cannot collect from his insurer for his noneconomic losses.

c. Tom can sue the at-fault party for his economic losses that exceed the $20,000 paid by his insurer—the additional $10,000. To recover any additional losses, he must first prove that the other driver was at fault for the accident.

d. Because Tom's economic losses ($30,000) are below the $50,000 monetary threshold in this modified no-fault state, he cannot sue the at-fault party for his noneconomic losses.

Educational Objective 3

3-1. Two types of programs that provide automobile insurance for high-risk drivers are voluntary market programs and residual market programs.

3-2. Insurers of high-risk drivers in the voluntary market accept their own applications, service their policies, pay their claims and expenses, and retain full responsibility for their own underwriting results. Insurers of high-risk drivers in the residual market may accept applications and service policies, but responsibility for underwriting results is usually transferred to a pool or shared proportionally by all insurers in the market in one of several ways.

3-3. Under a state automobile insurance plan, all auto insurers doing business in the state are assigned their proportionate share of high-risk drivers based on the total volume of auto insurance written in the state.

3-4. The state JUA sets the insurance rates and approves the policy forms to be used for high-risk drivers. The JUA designates servicing insurers that settle claims of high-risk drivers.

3-5. These answers address questions regarding XYZ Auto Insurance.

a. XYZ accepts Mary's application and services her policy.

b. In servicing Mary's policy under the pool arrangement of the reinsurance facility, XYZ handles Bill's liability claim.

c. Because the state has a reinsurance facility, all private insurers doing business in the state share any underwriting losses that occur as a result of Bill's claim.

Educational Objective 4

4-1. These answers address questions regarding automobile insurance rating factors and why insurers use them:

a. Territorial factors include the location where the auto is used and garaged, road conditions, state safety laws, and the extent of traffic regulation. These factors affect the frequency and/or severity of loss.

b. Young drivers have less driving experience and tend to be involved in accidents more frequently than older drivers. Therefore, rates for younger drivers are often higher than those for more experienced drivers.

c. Young drivers who complete an approved driver education course (usually including road experience) often qualify for a premium discount. Drivers age fifty-five and older sometimes qualify for a premium discount for successfully completing defensive driver training courses. Driver training can help reduce the frequency and severity of auto losses.

d. A discount is often given to policyholders who have more than one auto under the same policy. Two or more autos owned by the same insured are usually not driven as often as a single auto. It is less costly for the insurer to cover additional autos under the same contract, so savings may be passed to the insured.

e. This numerical ranking is based on the individual's financial history (similar to a credit score, but without income data) and is sometimes used to determine insurance rates. Research shows that insureds with low insurance scores submit more claims than insureds with high scores.

4-2. Insurers often divide auto insurance applicants into homogeneous classes (rating categories), such as "preferred," "standard," and "nonstandard," that reflect different levels of exposure to loss. Applicants who have good driving records and rating factors present minimal loss exposure and are categorized as preferred. Conversely, applicants who have poor driving records or rating factors present greater loss exposure and are categorized as nonstandard and charged higher rates.

4-3. Intense competition among insurers prompts regulators to monitor rates carefully to ensure adequacy and reasonableness. Regulators monitor rates primarily through insurers' rate filings.

4-4. These answers address questions regarding XYZ Insurance:

a. If a large number of applicants of the predominant ethnic origin had poor driving experience and/or numerous claims, a 70 percent discount on their rate would be unlikely to provide enough profit for the insurer to adequately pay its claims and expenses.

b. A 70 percent discount on rates based on the applicant's ethnic origin is unfairly discriminatory to all other applicants because an individual's ethnicity does not affect loss potential.

Direct Your Learning ▶▶

Personal Auto Policy: Liability, Med Pay, and UM Coverage

Educational Objectives

After learning the content of this assignment, you should be able to:

1. Summarize the sections of the Personal Auto Policy.

2. Identify the types of information typically contained on the Declarations page of the Personal Auto Policy.

3. Define the words and phrases included in the Definitions section of the Personal Auto Policy.

4. Summarize each of the provisions in Part A—Liability Coverage of the Personal Auto Policy.

5. Given a case describing an auto liability claim, determine whether Part A—Liability Coverage of the Personal Auto Policy would cover the claim and, if so, the amount the insurer would pay for the claim.

6. Summarize each of the provisions in Part B—Medical Payments Coverage of the Personal Auto Policy.

7. Given a case describing an auto medical payments claim, determine whether Part B—Medical Payments Coverage of the Personal Auto Policy would cover the claim and, if so, the amount the insurer would pay for the claim.

8. Summarize each of the provisions in Part C—Uninsured Motorists Coverage of the Personal Auto Policy.

9. Describe underinsured motorists insurance in terms of:

   - Its purpose

   - The ways in which it can vary by state

3

10. Given a case describing an uninsured motorists claim, determine whether Part C—Uninsured Motorists Coverage of the Personal Auto Policy would cover the claim and, if so, the amount the insurer would pay for the claim.

Outline

s.m.a.r.t. tips

Actively capture information by using the open space in the SMART Review Notes to write out key concepts. Putting information into your own words is an effective way to push that information into your memory.

Outline

▶ Part C—Uninsured Motorists Coverage

A. Insuring Agreement

 1. Insured Persons

 2. Uninsured Motor Vehicles

B. Exclusions

 1. Owned But Not Insured Vehicle

 2. Owned Vehicle With Primary UM Coverage in Other Policy

 3. Claim Settlement That Prejudices Insurer's Right of Recovery

 4. Public or Livery Conveyance

 5. Vehicle Used Without Reasonable Belief of Being Entitled

 6. No Benefit to Workers Compensation or Disability Benefits Insurer

 7. Punitive Damages

 8. Personal Vehicle Sharing Program

C. Limit of Liability

D. Other Insurance

E. Arbitration

▶ UM/UIM Endorsements and State Variations

A. Purpose of Coverage

B. State Variations

 1. Mandatory or Optional Coverage

 2. Limits Trigger or Damages Trigger

 3. Stacking

▶ Part C—Uninsured Motorists Coverage Case Study

A. Case Facts

B. Case Analysis Tools

C. Determination of Coverage

D. Determination of Amounts Payable

For each assignment, you should define or describe each of the Key Words and Phrases and answer each of the Review and Application Questions.

Educational Objective 1
Summarize the sections of the Personal Auto Policy.

Review Questions

1-1. List the information found on the Declarations page of an Insurance Services Office, Inc. (ISO) Personal Auto Policy (PAP).

1-2. Identify the information contained in the Agreement and Definitions page of the PAP.

1-3. Contrast the coverage provided under Part A of the PAP with the coverage provided under Part D.

Application Question

1-4. At the renewal of his policy, George switched insurers for the PAP covering his family's vehicles. Explain how George can use the Declarations page to compare the new policy with the policy from the previous insurer.

Educational Objective 2

Identify the types of information typically contained on the Declarations page of the Personal Auto Policy.

Key Words and Phrases

Named insured

Policy period

Vehicle identification number (VIN)

Review Questions

2-1. Describe the policy period for a personal auto policy (PAP).

2-2. List the information that is included in the description of insured autos on the PAP.

2-3. Identify the rating information found on the PAP Declarations page that may lead to reduced premiums.

Application Question

2-4. Amy is completing an application for a PAP and is not sure how to answer the question regarding the garage location for her vehicle. Explain what this term means and how it is used on the PAP.

Educational Objective 3
Define the words and phrases included in the Definitions section of the Personal Auto Policy.

Key Words and Phrases

Collision coverage

Other than collision (OTC) coverage

Review Questions

3-1. Explain why some words or phrases included in the PAP are shown in quotation marks.

3-2. Explain how the definition of "you" and "your" provides coverage for a spouse of the named insured.

3-3. Describe the purpose of the "leased vehicles" definition in the PAP.

3-4. Describe the importance of the definition of "business" in the PAP.

Application Question

3-5. Janice lives in her own apartment and insures her car under a PAP. Her sisters, Dana and Louise, still live at home with their parents. Explain whether Dana and Louise are included as family members under Janice's auto coverage as defined in the PAP.

Educational Objective 4

Summarize each of the provisions in Part A—Liability Coverage of the Personal Auto Policy.

Key Words and Phrases

Compensatory damages

Split-limits basis

Single-limits basis

Prejudgment interest

Supplementary payments

Attachment

Postjudgment interest

Public or livery conveyance

Review Questions

4-1. Explain what occurs if the cost to defend an insured under the Personal Auto Policy (PAP) exceeds the policy limit of liability.

4-2. Describe the situation in which an insurer would pay the cost of a bail bond for an insured under a PAP.

4-3. Explain the intent behind the PAP exclusion that eliminates liability coverage for an insured while employed or engaged in the business of selling, repairing, servicing, storing, or parking vehicles designed for use mainly on public highways.

Application Question

4-4. Sara works as a maid for Charlie. Charlie insures his auto under a PAP. He asks Sara to accompany him to the grocery store. While en route, he drives the car into a pole, causing bodily injury to Sara. Workers compensation benefits are not required for domestic employees in the state where the accident occurred. Explain what liability coverage Charlie has for Sara's claims against him.

Educational Objective 5

Given a case describing an auto liability claim, determine whether Part A—Liability Coverage of the Personal Auto Policy would cover the claim and, if so, the amount the insurer would pay for the claim.

Application Question

5-1. Mark's car breaks down as he is getting ready to go out of state on vacation. He takes the car to his mechanic and learns that a required part for the repair will not arrive for a week. Mark leaves the car at the shop and rents a car to use on his vacation. While driving out of state, Mark is involved in an accident in which he unintentionally drives his rental vehicle into the rear of the vehicle in front of him. The driver of the other vehicle sustains a neck injury.

Mark's PAP has limits of 30/60/10. The state where the accident occurs has required liability limits of 50/100/25. Mark is found liable, and the other driver is awarded $45,000.

Will Mark's PAP provide coverage for this accident? If so, how much will his insurer pay?

Educational Objective 6

Summarize each of the provisions in Part B—Medical Payments Coverage of the Personal Auto Policy.

Review Questions

6-1. Describe the two classes of insureds covered by Part B of the Personal Auto Policy (PAP).

6-2. Describe the exception to the PAP Part B exclusion that eliminates coverage for injuries sustained by an insured while occupying a vehicle (other than a covered auto) that is owned by or available for the regular use of a family member.

6-3. Explain how a coverage issue is resolved in a claim from a driver who has Part B coverage under a PAP and who was injured while driving a borrowed vehicle whose owner also has Part B coverage under a PAP.

Application Question

6-4. Elizabeth's son, Sam, is a family member as defined in his mother's PAP. Although Sam is old enough to drive, after having been involved in several serious accidents, he has promised his mother that he will not drive. However, late one Saturday night, Sam becomes bored and decides to go for a drive. He takes his mother's car while she is sleeping. While driving, he strikes a parked car and is injured. Explain what medical expense coverage Sam may have under Elizabeth's PAP.

Educational Objective 7

Given a case describing an auto medical payments claim, determine whether Part B—Medical Payments Coverage of the Personal Auto Policy would cover the claim and, if so, the amount the insurer would pay for the claim.

Application Question

7-1. Nora is driving with her thirteen-year-old daughter, Amanda, on a snowy road on February 4, 20X0, when the car skids and hits a utility pole. Amanda has a broken tooth, and she is treated by her dentist immediately after the accident. The dentist caps the tooth, and the bill is $2,350. On June 16, 20X4, after her high school graduation, Amanda has a replacement cap put on the broken tooth because her teeth have grown since the accident. The bill for the replacement cap is $3,000. Nora had a PAP with $5,000 medical payments coverage per person.

Would Amanda's dental treatment be covered under Nora's PAP? If so, how much would the insurer pay?

Educational Objective 8
Summarize each of the provisions in Part C—Uninsured Motorists Coverage of the Personal Auto Policy.

Key Words and Phrases
Uninsured motor vehicle

Arbitration

Review Questions

8-1. Describe the four categories of criteria a vehicle must meet to be covered by Part C of the Personal Auto Policy (PAP).

8-2. Explain the purpose of the PAP Part C exclusion that eliminates uninsured motorists (UM) coverage for a claim that the insured settles without the insurer's consent if such a settlement prejudices the insurer's right to recover payment.

8-3. Describe the Part C policy provision that is intended to prevent "stacking" of UM payments under a policy that covers more than one car owned by the named insured.

8-4. Explain whether a decision resulting from arbitration, the dispute resolution method designated by Part C of the PAP, is binding upon both parties when the amount of damages agreed on exceeds the minimum limit for bodily injury specified by the state's financial responsibility law.

Application Question

8-5. Doug is employed as a delivery driver for a pizza restaurant. When delivering pizza, he uses his own vehicle, which is insured under his PAP. Doug is seriously injured during a pizza delivery when his car is struck from behind by a hit-and-run driver. The pizza restaurant's workers compensation insurer, Delmond Insurance, pays Doug for his medical expenses and lost wages. Delmond Insurance decides to seek reimbursement from Doug's PAP insurer under Part C of Doug's policy. Explain the basis of Delmond's claim and what will likely occur in Delmond's attempt to assert it.

Educational Objective 9

Describe underinsured motorists insurance in terms of:

- **Its purpose**
- **The ways in which it can vary by state**

Review Questions

9-1. Describe the conditions in which underinsured motorists (UIM) coverage applies.

9-2. Aside from using ISO's Underinsured Motorists Coverage Endorsement (PP 03 11), explain how states can provide UIM coverage as a supplement to the UM coverage in the Personal Auto Policy (PAP).

9-3. Describe the key criterion that determines when a UIM endorsement with a limits trigger applies.

Application Question

9-4. Carol and Richard each live in a state that applies a damages trigger to a UIM endorsement. Carol has an auto liability policy with a $75,000 UIM limit. Richard purchased auto liability coverage with a $125,000 single limit. Richard causes an auto accident in which Carol is injured.

   a. Explain how Carol's UIM coverage will be affected if her damages amount to $200,000.

   b. Explain how Carol's UIM coverage will be affected if her damages amount to $100,000.

Educational Objective 10

Given a case describing an uninsured motorists claim, determine whether Part C—Uninsured Motorists Coverage of the Personal Auto Policy would cover the claim and, if so, the amount the insurer would pay for the claim.

Application Question

10-1. Barbara is driving her son Noah and his friend David to a school event when her vehicle is struck by a drunk driver who is uninsured and has no assets. David sustains a neck fracture that requires surgery. His medical bills are $157,000. Barbara has UIM coverage of $100,000 per person under her PAP. David's parents also have UIM coverage of $100,000 under their PAP.

Is there coverage for David's medical costs under either Barbara's PAP or David's parents' PAP or both? If so, how much will the insurer(s) pay?

Answers to Assignment 3 Questions

NOTE: These answers are provided to give students a basic understanding of acceptable types of responses. They often are not the only valid answers and are not intended to provide an exhaustive response to the questions.

Educational Objective 1

1-1. The Declarations page of the PAP can include the name and mailing address of both the insurer and the named insured; the policy period; and the name and address of the producer, if applicable. It also may include a description of the covered autos, limits of liability, premium and rating information, and any endorsements added to the policy.

1-2. The Agreement and Definitions page of the PAP includes a general agreement stating that the insurer is providing the coverage subject to payment of premium and to the terms of the policy. Definitions are also provided for words and phrases used throughout the policy.

1-3. Part A provides liability coverage and protects the insured against claims for bodily injury or property damage arising out of the operation of an auto. Part D of the PAP covers physical damage to a covered auto and includes collision and other than collision coverages.

1-4. When comparing the two policies, George can look at the Declarations page of each policy to review the dates of coverage, the descriptions of covered autos, limits of liability, endorsement listings, and premiums in order to determine whether any changes have been made and whether the information is accurate.

Educational Objective 2

2-1. The policy period starts at 12:01 a.m. standard time at the address of the policyholder on the date the policy becomes effective and ends at 12:01 a.m. standard time on the date the policy expires.

2-2. The description of insured autos usually includes the year, make, model, and vehicle identification number (VIN) of each covered vehicle. The description may also include the body type, annual mileage, use of the vehicle, and date of purchase.

2-3. Rating information that could qualify for premium discounts and lead to reduced premiums include the insured's having multiple cars insured under the policy, passing a driver training or defensive driving course, achieving a good scholastic record, or having a vehicle with passive restraints or anti-theft devices.

2-4. The garage location is the place where the auto is principally parked overnight. This location is used for rating purposes when calculating the premium for the policy.

Educational Objective 3

3-1. When a word or phrase is shown in quotation marks, this means that the definition for that word or phrase is included in the definitions section of the policy and that those definitions apply to the entire policy.

3-2. The words "you" and "your" also include an unnamed spouse of the named insured—provided that the spouse is a resident of the same household. When an unnamed spouse of the named insured moves out of the household but remains married to the insured, the spouse is considered "you" for another ninety days or until the policy expires—whichever comes first. Coverage ceases if the spouse is named on another policy.

3-3. The definition of "leased vehicles" clarifies what the policy includes when it refers to an owned auto. A leased private passenger auto, pickup, or van is deemed to be an owned auto if it is leased under a written agreement for a continuous period of at least six months.

3-4. The definition of "business" is important in understanding exclusions that apply to the coverage parts in the PAP.

3-5. Neither Dana nor Louise would be included in the definition of family members under Janice's auto coverage because they do not reside in the same household as Janice. The PAP defines a family member as a person who is related to the named insured or spouse by blood, marriage, or adoption and who resides in the named insured's household.

Educational Objective 4

4-1. If the cost to defend an insured under the PAP exceeds the policy limit of liability, the insurer agrees to defend the insured and pay all legal costs the insured may incur in a liability suit—even if the combined costs exceed the limit of liability. In other words, the insurer is obligated to pay defense costs in addition to the policy limits.

4-2. Regarding the situation in which an insurer would pay the cost of a bail bond for an insured under a PAP, the cost of a bail bond is covered under the PAP's Supplementary Payments provision. The insurer agrees to pay up to $250 for the cost of a bail bond (bail bond premium) required because of an accident that results in bodily injury or property damage covered by the policy.

4-3. The intent behind this PAP exclusion is to exclude a loss exposure that should be covered by a commercial auto policy, such as a garage policy, purchased by the owner of the business.

4-4. The PAP excludes liability coverage for bodily injury to an employee of an insured who is injured during the course of employment. Sara is employed by Charlie, the insured, and was injured during the course of her employment. However, an exception to this exclusion is injury to a domestic employee in the course of employment when workers compensation benefits are not required. Therefore, despite the exclusion, Charlie's PAP should provide coverage for Sara's liability claim against him.

Educational Objective 5

5-1. Mark's PAP will provide coverage for this accident. Mark is found liable for an unintentional rear-end collision. The PAP definition of "your covered auto" includes any auto that the named insured does not own while used as a temporary substitute for any other covered auto that is out of normal use because of its breakdown or repair. Mark is using a rental auto because his car is in the shop for repair following its breakdown.

The PAP also contains an Out of State Coverage provision that applies when an auto accident occurs in a state other than the one in which the covered auto is principally garaged. If the accident occurs in a state that has a financial responsibility law or a similar law that requires higher liability limits than the limits shown in the declarations, the PAP automatically provides the higher required limits for that accident. In this case, the liability limits in the state of the accident are higher than those in Mark's state. Mark's PAP will provide coverage for the $45,000 award, which is within the required liability limits of the accident state.

Educational Objective 6

6-1. Part B covers two classes of insureds:

- The named insured and "family members" (as defined in the PAP) are covered for their medical expenses if they are injured while occupying a motor vehicle or as pedestrians when struck by a motor vehicle designed for use mainly on public roads.

- Any other person while occupying a covered auto.

6-2. The exclusion that eliminates coverage for injuries sustained by an insured while occupying a vehicle (other than a covered auto) that is owned by or available for the regular use of a family member does not apply to the named insured and spouse occupying such a vehicle.

6-3. Regarding how a coverage issue is resolved in a claim from a driver who has Part B coverage under a PAP and who was injured while driving a borrowed vehicle whose owner also has Part B coverage under a PAP, for the driver of the nonowned vehicle, the driver's own PAP is excess over any other collectible auto insurance that pays medical or funeral expenses, including the PAP of the owner of the vehicle.

6-4. Part B of the PAP contains an exclusion that eliminates coverage if an insured sustains an injury while using a vehicle without a reasonable belief that he is entitled to do so. Taking his mother's car while she was sleeping and having made a previous promise that he would not drive would appear to place Sam within the application of this exclusion and preclude coverage for his injuries in this accident. However, the medical payments exclusion does not apply to a family member who uses an owned auto of the named insured. For insurance purposes, it is assumed that a family member has permission to use another family member's car. Therefore, Sam's medical expenses should be covered by his mother's PAP within the limits of her policy.

Educational Objective 7

7-1. Amanda is Nora's family member, and dental treatment qualifies as a medical expense. The expense for the treatment she receives immediately after the accident would be covered. However, the insurer agrees to pay only those expenses incurred for services rendered within three years from the date of the accident. Therefore, the expenses for the replacement cap that were incurred four years later would not be covered. The insurer would pay $2,350.

Educational Objective 8

8-1. To be covered by Part C, a vehicle must be a land vehicle or trailer that meets any of these criteria:

- No bodily injury liability insurance or bond applies to the vehicle at the time of the accident.

- A bodily injury liability policy or bond is in force, but the limit for bodily injury is less than the minimum amount required by the state's financial responsibility law.

- The vehicle is a hit-and-run vehicle whose owner or operator cannot be identified.

- A bodily injury policy or bond applies at the time of the accident, but the insurance or bonding company (a) denies coverage or (b) is or becomes insolvent.

8-2. The purpose of this exclusion is to protect the insurer's right to assert a subrogation action against the party who is legally responsible for the insured's injuries.

8-3. The terms in the limit of liability provision are intended to prevent stacking. The terms state that the limits shown in the declarations are the most that will be paid regardless of the number of insured persons, claims made, vehicles or premiums shown in the declarations, or vehicles involved in the accident.

8-4. If the amount agreed on in arbitration exceeds the statutory limit, either party can demand the right to a trial within sixty days of the arbitrators' decision. Otherwise, the arbitrators' decision is binding.

8-5. In some states, if an injured employee receives workers compensation benefits, the workers compensation insurer has a legal right to recover the amount of the benefits from a negligent third party through subrogation. If an employee receives workers compensation benefits for an injury involving an uninsured, at-fault driver, the workers compensation insurer could sue the driver or attempt to make a claim under the injured employee's UM coverage, which is what Delmond Insurance is attempting to do. However, Part C of the PAP contains an exclusion that prevents any insurer from benefiting directly or indirectly under a workers compensation law. That exclusion will likely prevent Delmond from obtaining reimbursement under Doug's PAP UM coverage.

Educational Objective 9

9-1. Underinsured motorists (UIM) coverage applies when a negligent driver is insured for at least the minimum required financial responsibility limits but the policy's liability limits are insufficient to pay the insured's damages.

9-2. Aside from using ISO's Underinsured Motorists Coverage Endorsement (PP 03 11), states can provide coverage as a supplement to the UM coverage in the PAP by using either a state-specific UIM endorsement or a single, state-specific endorsement providing both UM and UIM coverages that replaces the UM coverage of the standard PAP.

9-3. The key criterion for UIM protection with a limits trigger is that the liability limits of the other party's policy are less than the insured's UIM limits.

9-4. These answers address questions regarding Carol's UIM coverage:

a. If Carol's damages amount to $200,000, her UIM coverage will be triggered because Richard's policy limit is less than Carol's damages.

▶▶

b. If Carol's damages amount to $100,000, her UIM coverage will not be triggered because her damages are less than Richard's limit.

Educational Objective 10

10-1. Barbara's PAP is primary coverage because she was the driver of the vehicle. Her insurer will pay the UIM limit of $100,000. There is excess coverage under David's parents' PAP because he is a family member. Their insurer will pay $57,000.

Direct Your Learning

PAP: Physical Damage, Duties After an Accident, Endorsements

Educational Objectives

After learning the content of this assignment, you should be able to:

1. Summarize each of the provisions in Part D—Coverage for Damage to Your Auto of the Personal Auto Policy.

2. Given a case describing an auto physical damage claim, determine whether Part D—Coverage for Damage to Your Auto of the Personal Auto Policy would cover the claim and, if so, the amount the insurer would pay for the claim.

3. Describe the insured's duties following a covered auto accident or loss as shown in Part E of the Personal Auto Policy.

4. Summarize each of the general provisions in Part F of the Personal Auto Policy.

5. Describe the Personal Auto Policy endorsements that are used to handle common auto loss exposures.

6. Describe the Personal Auto Endorsements that are used to handle exposures related to transportation network companies.

7. Given a case describing an auto claim, determine whether the Personal Auto Policy would cover the claim and, if so, the amount the insurer would pay for the claim.

Outline

▶ **Part D—Coverage for Damage to Your Auto**
  A. Insuring Agreement
    1. Collision Coverage
    2. Other Than Collision Coverage
    3. Nonowned Autos
    4. Deductibles
  B. Transportation Expenses
  C. Exclusions
    1. Public or Livery Conveyance
    2. Wear and Tear, Freezing, Breakdown, and Road Damage to Tires
    3. Radioactive Contamination or War
    4. Electronic Equipment
    5. Media and Accessories
    6. Government Destruction or Confiscation
    7. Trailer, Camper Body, or Motor Home
    8. Nonowned Auto Used Without Reasonable Belief of Being Entitled
    9. Radar and Laser Detection Equipment
    10. Customizing Equipment
    11. Nonowned Auto Used in Garage Business
    12. Racing
    13. Rental Vehicles
    14. Personal Vehicle Sharing Program
  D. Limit of Liability
  E. Payment of Loss
  F. No Benefit to Bailee
  G. Other Sources of Recovery
  H. Appraisal
▶ **Part D—Coverage for Damage to Your Auto Case Study**
  A. Case Facts
  B. Case Analysis Tools
  C. Determination of Coverage
  D. Determination of Amounts Payable

▶ **Part E—Duties After an Accident or Loss**
  A. General Duties
  B. Additional Duties for Uninsured Motorists Coverage
  C. Additional Duties for Physical Damage Coverage
▶ **Part F—General Provisions**
  A. Bankruptcy of Insured
  B. Changes in the Policy
  C. Fraud
  D. Legal Action Against the Insurer
  E. Insurer's Right to Recover Payment
  F. Policy Period and Territory
  G. Termination
    1. Cancellation
    2. Nonrenewal
    3. Automatic Termination
    4. Other Termination Provisions
  H. Transfer of Insured's Interest in the Policy
  I. Two or More Auto Policies
▶ **Common Endorsements to the Personal Auto Policy**
  A. Miscellaneous Type Vehicle Endorsement
  B. Snowmobile Endorsement
  C. Trailer/Camper Body Coverage (Maximum Limit of Liability)
  D. Extended Non-Owned Coverage—Vehicles Furnished or Available for Regular Use
  E. Named Non-Owner Coverage
  F. Auto Loan/Lease Coverage
  G. Limited Mexico Coverage
  H. Excess Electronic Equipment Coverage
  I. Coverage for Damage to Your Auto (Maximum Limit of Liability)
  J. Optional Limits Transportation Expenses Coverage
  K. Towing and Labor Costs Coverage

s.m.a.r.t. tips   The SMART Online Practice Exams can be tailored to cover specific assignments, so you can focus your studies on topics you want to master.

▶▶

Outline

▶ **Personal Auto Endorsements for Transportation Network Exposures**

   A. Public or Livery Conveyance Exclusion Endorsement

   B. Transportation Network Driver Coverage (No Passenger) Endorsement

   C. Limited Transportation Network Driver Coverage (No Passenger) Endorsement

▶ **Personal Auto Coverage Case Study**

   A. Case Facts

   B. Case Analysis Tools

   C. Determination of Coverage

   D. Determination of Amounts Payable

For each assignment, you should define or describe each of the Key Words and Phrases and answer each of the Review and Application Questions.

Educational Objective 1

Summarize each of the provisions in Part D—Coverage for Damage to Your Auto of the Personal Auto Policy.

Key Words and Phrases

Physical damage coverages

Deductible

Transportation expenses

Actual cash value (ACV)

Appraisal

Review Questions

1-1. Explain John's options for collecting damages if he has collision coverage for his car and another driver causes an accident that damages John's car.

1-2. Explain how often an insured can drive a rented or borrowed auto and expect his or her auto physical damage insurance to cover the vehicle.

1-3. List three reasons for deductibles in auto physical damage coverage.

1-4. Explain whether, if an insured decides to race his sports car against the driver of another car on a city street, damage to his car resulting from a collision that occurs during this activity would be excluded under his PAP collision coverage.

Application Question

1-5. Jack rents a car from XYZ Rental Car Agency. He declines the damage waiver offered by XYZ at a substantial extra cost. While driving the rental car, Jack is involved in an auto accident with another car. Who is at fault is being contested, but, in the meantime, the rental car is not available to be rented while it is being repaired. XYZ has demanded reimbursement from Jack for its loss of the income the car would have earned in rental fees of $40 per day. Will Jack's PAP collision coverage for his covered auto help him in this situation and, if so, to what extent?

Educational Objective 2

Given a case describing an auto physical damage claim, determine whether Part D—Coverage for Damage to Your Auto of the Personal Auto Policy would cover the claim and, if so, the amount the insurer would pay for the claim.

Application Questions

2-1. Lucia has a PAP with coverage for other than collision (OTC) loss that is subject to a $200 deductible. However, she did not purchase collision coverage and is not insured for those losses. What dollar amount, if any, will Lucia's insurer pay under her PAP for each of these losses? If a loss is not covered or not fully covered, explain why. Treat each loss separately.

   a. Lucia parks her car at the grocery store and goes shopping. She returns just in time to see another vehicle strike her car and then quickly leave. Assume that the state where Lucia's car is principally garaged does not allow uninsured motorists property damage coverage. Her mechanic estimates that the repairs will cost $1,000.

b. Lucia's factory-installed car radio valued at $400 was stolen from her car.

2-2. Tony has a PAP with coverage for OTC loss that is subject to a $500 deductible. After enjoying a night out at the movies with his friends, Tony discovers that his car has been stolen from the theatre parking lot. He immediately reports the loss to the police and to his insurer. The next morning, Tony rents a substitute auto for $40 a day. Thirty-six hours after the theft, the police report that they have found the car intact. Tony determines that the only items stolen were his compact discs (CDs), valued at approximately $500.

a. What dollar amount, if any, will Tony's PAP pay for his rented auto?

b. What dollar amount, if any, will Tony's PAP pay for the rented auto if his car was recovered after having been missing for a total of seven days?

Educational Objective 3

Describe the insured's duties following a covered auto accident or loss as shown in Part E of the Personal Auto Policy.

Key Word or Phrase

Proof of loss

Review Questions

3-1. List the seven general duties a person seeking coverage under the PAP must perform after an accident or a loss.

3-2. Describe the details a person seeking coverage under the PAP should include when notifying the insurer that an accident or a loss has occurred.

3-3. Describe two additional duties required if the insured is seeking payment under Coverage C—Uninsured Motorists Coverage of the PAP.

3-4. Part E of a PAP states the general duties that the insured must perform after an accident or a loss. Additional duties are required if the insured is seeking payment under Part D—Coverage for Damage to Your Auto.

   a.   Explain why it is important for insureds to perform the duties after a loss as outlined in Part E of the PAP.

b. Describe the three additional duties required if the insured is seeking payment under Part D of the PAP.

Educational Objective 4

Summarize each of the general provisions in Part F of the Personal Auto Policy.

Key Words and Phrases

Liberalization Clause

Policy termination

Cancellation

Review Questions

4-1. Briefly describe each of the general provisions in Part F of the PAP:

a. Bankruptcy of the Insured

b. Policy Period and Territory

c. Two or More Policies

4-2. Identify four changes an insured can make during the policy period that can result in a premium increase or decrease.

4-3. Describe the obligations that an insured must fulfill before he or she can sue the insurer.

4-4. List the three reasons for which an insurer can cancel a policy that has been in force for sixty or more days.

Application Question

4-5. Explain how the PAP would respond in the following situations based on the provisions contained in Part F of the policy.

    a. The insured deliberately burns his car and submits a claim under the policy's physical damage coverage.

    b. Henry has replaced his current auto insurance policy with a new insurer. What must he do to cancel his original auto policy, which was issued by a different insurer?

Educational Objective 5

Describe the Personal Auto Policy endorsements that are used to handle common auto loss exposures.

Review Questions

5-1. Explain why an insured may want to include an optional passenger exclusion to a Miscellaneous Type Vehicle endorsement.

5-2. Explain why an insured would purchase an Extended Non-Owned Coverage—Vehicles Furnished or Available for Regular Use endorsement.

5-3. Describe how a stated amount of insurance may not provide coverage for that amount when a Coverage for Damage to Your Auto endorsement has been added to the PAP.

Educational Objective 6
Describe the Personal Auto Endorsements that are used to handle exposures related to transportation network companies.

Key Words and Phrases
Transportation network company

Liability coverage

Medical payments coverage

Review Questions

6-1. Describe how Insurance Services Office, Inc. (ISO) has clarified when coverage under a driver's personal auto policy (PAP) ends in regards to transportation network company (TNC) drivers.

6-2. Explain the ISO Public or Livery Conveyance Exclusion Endorsement.

6-3. Explain the similarities and differences between the Transportation Network Driver Coverage (No Passenger) endorsement and the Limited Transportation Network Driver Coverage (No Passenger) endorsement.

Educational Objective 7

Given a case describing an auto claim, determine whether the Personal Auto Policy would cover the claim and, if so, the amount the insurer would pay for the claim.

Application Question

7-1. John and Marcia are on a winter vacation with their three children. Their sons, Neil and Henry, rent snowmobiles and participate in an unofficial snowmobile race with some of the other teenagers staying at the same lodge. Henry hits a fence with the snowmobile he is driving. Fortunately, Henry is not injured, but he causes $3,200 in damage to the fence.

While their sons are on snowmobiles, John drives to the ski area with Marcia and their daughter, Lauren. As they are rounding the curve of a mountain road, a vehicle driven by Alex crosses the center line and hits their van. The van goes over the side of the road. John, Marcia, and Lauren are all injured and taken to the hospital by ambulance. John, Marcia, and Lauren sue Alex for $250,000 for John, $100,000 for Marcia, and $300,000 for Lauren—a total of $650,000. They agree to settle for $500,000.

John has a PAP with a snowmobile endorsement that has a limit of liability of $50,000. Alex has a PAP with a $500,000 limit of liability for each occurrence.

What losses will be covered by John's and Alex's PAP policies and in what amounts?

Answers to Assignment 4 Questions

NOTE: These answers are provided to give students a basic understanding of acceptable types of responses. They often are not the only valid answers and are not intended to provide an exhaustive response to the questions.

Educational Objective 1

1-1. John can collect either from the other driver (or the driver's insurer) or from his own insurer. If John collects from his insurer, that insurer has the right to recover payment from the driver (or the driver's insurer). This recovery is referred to as subrogation.

1-2. The vehicle would be covered if driven occasionally by the insured. However, if the insured regularly drives the rented or borrowed vehicle, or if it is made available for the insured's regular use, the insured's coverage will not apply.

1-3. Insurers require deductibles in auto physical damage coverage for several reasons:

- To reduce small claims

- To hold down premiums

- To encourage insureds to be careful in protecting their cars against damage or theft

1-4. The damage to the insured's car from racing would probably not be excluded. Loss to a covered auto is excluded if the auto is damaged while located in a facility designed for racing if the auto is being used to prepare for, practice for, or compete in any prearranged racing or speed contest. It appears that this race was not prearranged.

1-5. Part D of Jack's PAP provides coverage for transportation expenses. Under this provision, the rental car is covered as a nonowned auto, and the rental company's lost income while the car is being repaired is covered. However, the transportation expenses are limited to a maximum of $20 per day and $600 for each covered loss. Also, although transportation expenses do not have a dollar-amount deductible, they are subject to a twenty-four-hour waiting period. Therefore, Jack's insurer would pay only $20 a day for XYZ's lost income, and the first day's loss would not be paid. Jack should also be aware that, at $20 per day and a maximum of $600, he has only thirty days of coverage ($600 divided by $20).

Educational Objective 2

2-1. These answers address questions about Luica's PAP:

a. In order for Lucia's PAP to cover these repairs, she would need collision coverage. Because Lucia has only other than collision coverage, her insurer will not cover the expense to repair her auto.

b. Because Lucia's radio was factory-installed, it is covered (less the deductible). So her insurer will pay $200 ($400 minus $200) for the loss.

2-2. These answers address questions about Tony's PAP:

a. Tony's PAP imposes a two-day waiting period before transportation expense reimbursement begins. Because his car was recovered thirty-six hours after the theft, Tony's insurer will not cover the expense for the rental car.

b. Although the cost of renting a temporary substitute auto is insured under the Transportation Expenses coverage of Tony's PAP, that coverage is limited to $20 a day, not to exceed a maximum of $600. (The deductible does not apply to the Transportation Expense coverage.) The car was missing for a total of seven days. However, since the claim involves a total theft of the car, there is a two-day waiting period. Therefore, Tony will receive reimbursement of $100—$20 per day for his transportation expenses for five days—to offset the $280 he paid for the rental car.

Educational Objective 3

3-1. A person seeking coverage under the PAP must perform seven duties:

- Provide prompt notification of the details of the accident or loss to the insurer

- Cooperate with the insurer in the investigation, settlement, or defense of any claim or suit

- Submit copies of notices or legal papers in connection with the accident or loss to the insurer

- Agree to submit to a physical examination if requested by the insurer

- Agree to be examined under oath if required by the insurer

- Authorize the insurer to obtain medical reports and other pertinent records

- Submit a proof of loss when required by the insurer

3-2. The notification should include details such as how, when, and where the accident happened, as well as the names and addresses of any injured persons and witnesses.

3-3. A person seeking benefits under Uninsured Motorists Coverage must perform two additional duties:

- Promptly notify the police if a hit-and-run driver is involved

- Send a copy of the legal papers to the insurance company if the person seeking coverage sues the uninsured motorist

3-4. These answers address questions regarding Parts D and E of a PAP:

a. It is important for insureds to perform the duties after a loss as outlined in Part E because if the insured does not perform them and this failure is prejudicial to the insurer, the insurer has no obligation to provide coverage and to pay for the loss.

b. There are three additional duties required if the insured is seeking payment under Part D of the PAP:

   • The person seeking coverage must take reasonable steps after a loss to protect a covered auto or nonowned auto and its equipment from further loss.

   • If a covered auto or nonowned auto is stolen, the person seeking coverage must promptly notify the police of the theft.

   • The person seeking coverage must permit the insurer to inspect and appraise the damaged property before its repair or disposal.

Educational Objective 4

4-1. These answers address questions regarding the general provisions in Part F of the PAP:

   a. This provision states that if the insured declares bankruptcy or becomes insolvent, the insurer is not relieved of any obligations under the policy.

   b. According to this provision, coverage applies only to accidents and losses that occur during the policy period shown on the declarations page. The policy territory includes the United States, U.S. territories and possessions, Puerto Rico, and Canada. The policy also applies to a covered auto while being transported among ports of the U.S., Puerto Rico, or Canada. Coverage does not apply anywhere outside the policy territory.

   c. According to this provision, if two or more auto policies issued to the named insured by the same insurer apply to the same accident, the insurer's maximum limit of liability is the highest applicable limit of liability under any one policy.

4-2. Changes an insured can make during the policy period that can result in a premium increase or decrease include changes in:

   • The number, type, or use of insured vehicles

   • The operators using insured vehicles

   • The place of principal garaging of insured vehicles

   • The coverage provided, deductibles, or limits of liability

4-3. No legal action can be brought against the insurer until the insured has fully complied with all of the policy terms. In addition, under Part A—Liability Coverage, no legal action can be brought against the insurer unless the insurer agrees in writing that the insured has an obligation to pay damages or the amount of the insurer's obligation has been finally determined by a judgment after a trial.

4-4. These are three reasons for which an insurer can cancel a policy that has been in force for sixty or more days:

   • The premium has not been paid.

   • The driver's license of an insured has been suspended or revoked during the policy period (or since the last annual anniversary of the original effective date if the policy is for other than one year).

   • The policy has been obtained by a material misrepresentation.

4-5. These answers address questions regarding how the PAP would respond based on provisions contained in Part F of the policy:

    a. Because the PAP contains a fraud provision stating that no coverage exists for any insured who makes fraudulent statements or engages in fraudulent conduct in connection with any accident or loss for which a claim is made, the insurer would not be obligated to pay this claim.

    b. To comply with the cancellation provision, Henry can cancel the original policy anytime during the policy period by returning the policy to the insurer or by giving advance written notice of the date the cancellation is to become effective.

Educational Objective 5

5-1. A motorcycle owner who never carries passengers can elect this exclusion in exchange for a lower premium.

5-2. The unendorsed Personal Auto Policy (PAP) excludes liability and medical payments coverage for vehicles furnished or made available for the regular use of the named insured and family members. This exclusion can be eliminated by adding the Extended Non-Owned Coverage—Vehicles Furnished or Available for Regular Use (PP 03 06 01 05) endorsement to the PAP. The endorsement provides liability coverage for any vehicle furnished or available for the regular use of the named individual and for family members who are indicated in the schedule. For example, if Alice is furnished with a company car by her employer, this endorsement would provide liability and/or medical payments coverage on an excess basis.

5-3. Even though the endorsement indicates a stated amount of insurance, it may not provide coverage for that amount in the event of a total loss to the vehicle. Rather, the insurer's maximum limit of liability for a covered loss is limited to the lowest of three values: the stated amount shown in the schedule or in the declarations; the actual cash value of the stolen or damaged property; or the amount necessary to repair or replace the property with other property of like kind and quality.

If, for example, the stated amount of insurance is less than the vehicle's actual cash value or the amount necessary to repair or replace the property, the stated amount is used as the basis of the loss settlement. However, if the stated amount of insurance is greater than the vehicle's actual cash value or the amount necessary to repair or replace the property, the lower amount is the basis for payment. In any case, the amount paid is reduced by any applicable deductible shown in the endorsement schedule or policy declarations.

Educational Objective 6

6-1. To clarify when coverage under a driver's PAP ends and to address potential coverage gaps, ISO has developed endorsements to the PAP.

6-2. ISO's Public or Livery Conveyance Exclusion Endorsement reinforces the public or livery conveyance exclusion in the PAP, which excludes coverage when a personal auto is used to transport people for a fee (for example, as a taxi). This endorsement adds a "transportation network platform" definition and explains that the exclusion applies to any period of time the insured has logged in to such a platform as a driver, whether or not a passenger is in the vehicle.

6-3. The Limited Transportation Network Driver Coverage (No Passenger) endorsement is similar to the Transportation Network Driver Coverage endorsement; both provide coverage when the insured is logged in to a transportation network platform but has not yet picked up a passenger. The limited version's coverage ends once the driver accepts a passenger, which occurs before the passenger enters the vehicle. The Transportation Network Driver Coverage (No Passenger) endorsement ends when a passenger enters the vehicle. Both versions exclude coverage when a passenger is occupying the vehicle.

Educational Objective 7

7-1. The $500,000 settlement for John, Marcia, and Lauren will be covered by Alex's PAP. He was liable because he crossed the center line, and his insurer settled for the policy limits.

John's PAP will not cover the damages from Henry's snowmobile accident because racing is excluded under the snowmobile endorsement.

B

Direct Your Learning

Homeowners Property Coverage

Educational Objectives

After learning the content of this assignment, you should be able to:

1. Describe how individuals and families can use the Insurance Services Office, Inc., (ISO) 2011 Homeowners insurance program to address their personal risk management needs.

2. Describe the Homeowners 3—Special Form (HO-3) in terms of:

   - Its structure and the coverages it provides

   - The role of endorsements in modifying it

   - The factors considered in rating it

3. Describe what is insured by each of these coverages contained in the 2011 Homeowners 3—Special Form (HO-3) policy:

   - Coverage A—Dwelling

   - Coverage B—Other Structures

   - Coverage C—Personal Property

   - Coverage D—Loss of Use

   - Additional Coverages

4. Describe what is covered and what is excluded by these provisions in the 2011 Homeowners 3—Special Form (HO-3) policy:

   - Perils Insured Against for Coverages A and B

   - Perils Insured Against for Coverage C

   - Section I—Exclusions

5. Summarize each of the 2011 Homeowners 3—Special Form (HO-3) policy provisions in Section I—Conditions.

5

6. Given a scenario describing a homeowners property claim, determine whether the 2011 HO-3 policy Section I—Property Coverages would cover the claim and, if so, the amount the insurer would pay for the claim.

Outline

study **tips**   **When reviewing for your exam, remember to allot time for frequent breaks.**

For each assignment, you should define or describe each of the Key Words and Phrases and answer each of the Review and Application Questions.

Educational Objective 1

Describe how individuals and families can use the Insurance Services Office, Inc., (ISO) 2011 Homeowners insurance program to address their personal risk management needs.

Key Word or Phrase

Functional replacement cost

Review Questions

1-1. Identify the three general categories into which the parties eligible for coverage under the Insurance Services Office, Inc. (ISO) 2011 Homeowners (HO) insurance program fall.

1-2. Describe the coverage provided by the HO-2 Broad Form.

1-3. Contrast the coverage provided by the HO-2 with the coverage provided by the HO-3.

1-4. Describe the coverage provided by the HO-4—Contents Broad Form.

1-5. Identify the coverage form that provides the broadest available coverage for a homeowner's home and contents.

1-6. For whose risk management needs is the HO-6—Unit-Owners Form designed?

1-7. Describe the coverage provided by the HO-8—Modified Coverage Form.

Educational Objective 2

Describe the Homeowners 3—Special Form (HO-3) in terms of:

- **Its structure and the coverages it provides**
- **The role of endorsements in modifying it**
- **The factors considered in rating it**

Review Questions

2-1. Identify the primary components of the Insurance Services Office, Inc. (ISO) Homeowners 3—Special Form (HO-3).

2-2. Give examples of questions that the declarations answer about the insured, the property covered, and the limits of coverage in the HO-3.

2-3. Explain the purpose of the HO-3 insuring agreement.

2-4. Describe the information that is included in HO-3 Section I.

2-5. Identify the ways in which endorsements can alter the HO-3.

2-6. Give examples of factors that influence the HO-3's base premium.

Educational Objective 3

Describe what is insured by each of these coverages contained in the 2011 Homeowners 3—Special Form (HO-3) policy:

- Coverage A—Dwelling
- Coverage B—Other Structures
- Coverage C—Personal Property
- Coverage D—Loss of Use
- Additional Coverages

Review Questions

3-1.   Identify three exclusions to coverage in the HO-3 under Coverage B—Other Structures.

3-2.   Describe the property to which Coverage C—Personal Property applies.

3-3.   Describe the personal property sublimits in the HO-3.

3-4. Identify the main reason that coverage is excluded for certain categories of personal property under Coverage C.

3-5. Name the three coverages provided under Coverage D.

Educational Objective 4

Describe what is covered and what is excluded by these provisions in the 2011 Homeowners 3—Special Form (HO-3) policy:

- **Perils Insured Against for Coverages A and B**
- **Perils Insured Against for Coverage C**
- **Section I—Exclusions**

Key Words and Phrases

Special form coverage

Named perils coverage

Review Questions

4-1. Explain why insured perils for Coverage A—Dwelling and Coverage B—Other Structures are grouped together in the Insurance Services Office, Inc. (ISO) Homeowners 3—Special Form (HO-3).

4-2. Describe the approach of HO-3 Section I—Property Coverages to perils insured against for direct physical loss under Coverages A and B and the intent of that approach.

4-3. Identify the type of property to which Coverage C under the HO-3 generally applies.

4-4. Explain why coverage for personal property under the HO-3 is not as broad as the open perils coverage for dwellings and other structures.

4-5. List the named perils covered under Coverage C of the HO-3 policy.

Application Questions

4-6. Julie has an HO-3 policy to insure her home, detached garage, and personal property. During a windstorm, a large tree branch fell through the roof and into Julie's living room, damaging the exterior and interior of her home, a sofa, and a coffee table. Rain that blew through the opening in the wall caused water damage to the dining room table. Considering Coverages A, B, and C, identify the appropriate coverages and explain whether the coverage(s) would insure her property against this peril (after any applicable deductible).

4-7. Assume that Julie has the same coverages as in the previous question. Julie's power company has been known to have power surges. One day, a power surge damaged Julie's central air conditioner, the components of her personal computer, and her projection television system. Identify the appropriate coverages and explain whether the coverage(s) would insure her property against this peril (after any applicable deductible).

Educational Objective 5

Summarize each of the 2011 Homeowners 3—Special Form (HO-3) policy provisions in Section I—Conditions.

Review Questions

5-1. Identify the purpose of the Insurance Services Office, Inc. (ISO) Homeowners 3—Special Form's (HO-3) Insurable Interest and Limit of Liability condition.

5-2. What was the purpose of the 2011 revision to the HO-3's Deductible condition?

5-3. List examples of the duties the insured must perform after a property loss under the HO-3.

5-4. Identify the purpose of the HO-3's Loss Settlement condition.

5-5. Summarize the procedure the HO-3's Appraisal condition outlines for resolving disputes between an insured and the insurer over the amount of a loss.

5-6. How does the HO-3 specify a loss be resolved that is covered by two or more insurance policies?

5-7. Identify the purpose of the HO-3's Our Option condition.

5-8. Describe the mortgagee rights the Mortgage Clause condition of the HO-3 establishes.

Application Question

5-9. Kim and Dan own a home. Kim has an HO-3 with a $100,000 Coverage A limit. Dan also purchased a homeowners policy with a $150,000 Coverage A limit for the home. A natural gas explosion destroyed the couple's home, which had a replacement cost of $200,000 at the time of the loss. After the explosion, they discover that two policies cover their home, with a total of $250,000 in coverage available. Calculate the amount that each policy will pay.

Educational Objective 6

Given a scenario describing a homeowners property claim, determine whether the 2011 HO-3 policy Section I— Property Coverages would cover the claim and, if so, the amount the insurer would pay for the claim.

Application Question

6-1. Steve and Kelly own a single-family home insured under an Insurance Services Office, Inc. (ISO) Homeowners 3—Special Form (HO-3) policy. One evening, a fire destroys the home's living room and several adjoining rooms. The structural damage to the home because of the fire is $75,000. The family's television is damaged. Cash ($375), which Steve kept in a countertop cookie jar for food-shopping trips, was also destroyed. Steve and Kelly are insured under an unendorsed HO-3 policy with a $300,000 dwelling limit and a $500 deductible. For the purposes of this case, assume that Steve and Kelly are in compliance with all policy conditions, including Coverage A replacement cost provisions.

   a. Identify the component of the HO-3 policy that would be used to determine whether coverage applies to Steve and Kelly at the time of the loss.

▶▶

b. Identify the component of the HO-3 policy that would be used to determine whether the policy applies to Steve and Kelly's loss.

c. Steve and Kelly's HO-3 contains a provision in the Special Limits of Liability portion of its Conditions section that states that a $200 limit applies to "money." Assuming that their loss is covered under their HO-3, how, if at all, would this condition affect the amount that Steve and Kelly receive from the insurer?

d. Assuming that their loss is covered under their HO-3 and accounting for the deductible, how much will Steve and Kelly receive for fire damage to their home under Coverage A?

e. Steve and Kelly's television, destroyed in the fire, was five years old but had a useful life of ten years. A new television equivalent to the destroyed model costs $600. The insurer's claims representative determines that it would cost $400 to repair the damage. Assuming that Steve and Kelly's loss is covered under their HO-3, how would compensation for the television be settled under Coverage C?

Answers to Assignment 5 Questions

NOTE: These answers are provided to give students a basic understanding of acceptable types of responses. They often are not the only valid answers and are not intended to provide an exhaustive response to the questions.

Educational Objective 1

1-1. The three general categories into which the parties eligible for coverage under the ISO 2011 HO insurance program fall are these:

   • Individuals and families who own a private home in which they reside

   • People who rent or lease the premises in which they reside

   • Individuals and families who own private condominium units used for residential purposes

1-2. The HO-2 Broad Form provides named perils coverage for dwellings, other structures, and personal property.

1-3. The HO-3 provides named perils coverage for personal property, as does the HO-2. The HO-3 is designed to meet the risk management needs of owner-occupants of dwellings who want broader coverage on their dwellings and other structures.

1-4. The HO-4—Contents Broad Form provides coverage for a tenant's personal property on a named perils basis.

1-5. A homeowner who desires the broadest available coverage for his or her home and contents, and is willing to pay the increased premium for it, should select the HO-5—Comprehensive Form.

1-6. The HO-6 is designed to meet the risk management needs of the owners of condominium units and cooperative apartment shares.

1-7. The HO-8—Modified Coverage Form provides coverage for a dwelling, other structures, and personal property on a limited, named perils basis.

Educational Objective 2

2-1. The HO-3 policy consists of these primary components:

   • Declarations

   • Agreement and Definitions

   • Section I—Property Coverages

   • Section II—Liability Coverages

   • Endorsements

2-2. The HO-3 declarations provide essential information about the insured, the property covered, and the limits of coverage provided by answering these questions:

- Who is the policyholder?
- Where is the policyholder's residence?
- What are the coverage limits?
- What is the premium?
- What is the Section I deductible?
- What is the effective date of the policy?
- Which forms and endorsements apply to the policy?
- Who is the mortgage holder?

2-3. The purpose of the HO-3 insuring agreement is to establish the basis for the contract and specify what the insurer and the insured will do. The insurer agrees to provide coverage, and the insured agrees to pay the premium and comply with the policy conditions.

2-4. HO-3 Section I specifies the property covered, the perils for which the property is covered, and the exclusions and conditions that affect property coverages and losses.

2-5. Endorsements to the HO-3 can increase or decrease limits, add or remove coverages, change definitions, clarify policy intent, or recognize specific characteristics that require a premium increase or decrease.

2-6. Factors that influence the HO-3's base premium include dwelling location, public protection class (classification used to rate the quality of community fire protection), construction factors, coverage amount, and the policy form selected.

Educational Objective 3

3-1. No coverage is provided for other structures that meet any of these criteria:

- A structure rented to anyone who is not a resident of the dwelling (unless it is rented as a private garage)
- A structure from which any business is conducted
- A structure used to store business property (unless the property is solely owned by an insured or a tenant of the dwelling and does not include gaseous or liquid fuel, other than fuel in a permanently installed fuel tank of a vehicle or craft parked or stored in the structure)

3-2. Coverage C—Personal Property applies to items the insured owns or uses, anywhere in the world. It can also cover loss of or damage to personal property of others while that property is on the residence premises if the named insured requests such coverage after a loss. Coverage C can also cover loss of or damage to personal property of a guest or residence employee while it is in any residence occupied by an insured.

3-3. Some categories of personal property are subject to sublimits, called special limits of liability, within the Coverage C limit. Items within these categories pose a higher-than-average risk of loss (for example, jewelry) or are types of property not contemplated in homeowners insurance premiums (for example, business property). The special limits for three personal property categories (jewelry and furs; firearms and related items; and silverware, goldware, platinumware, and pewterware) apply only when loss is caused by theft. The special limits for eight other categories of personal property apply when loss is caused by any covered peril.

3-4. In most cases, coverage is excluded for certain categories of personal property under Coverage C because these items are insured through policies other than a homeowners policy.

3-5. These are the three coverages provided under Coverage D:

- Additional living expense

- Fair rental value

- Loss of use due to civil authority

Educational Objective 4

4-1. Insured perils for Coverage A—Dwelling and Coverage B—Other Structures are grouped together because both coverages provide open perils coverage for real property items with similar exposures to loss.

4-2. Under the HO-3 Section I, a broad statement of coverage against direct physical loss under Coverages A and B is followed by a statement that lists the excluded perils. Any peril that is not listed in these exclusions is covered.

4-3. Coverage C under the HO-3 applies to the contents of a home and other personal property.

4-4. Regarding why coverage for personal property under the HO-3 is not as broad as the open perils coverage for dwellings and other structures, Coverage C applies on a named perils basis, meaning that coverage applies only if covered property is damaged as a result of a cause of loss named in the policy. While open perils and named perils cover many of the same causes of loss, open perils coverage sometimes includes causes of loss that are not among the named perils.

4-5. Coverage C named perils include these:

- Fire or lightning
- Windstorm or hail
- Explosion
- Riot or civil commotion
- Aircraft
- Vehicles
- Smoke
- Vandalism or malicious mischief
- Theft
- Falling objects
- Weight of ice, snow, or sleet
- Accidental discharge or overflow of water or steam
- Sudden and accidental tearing apart, cracking, burning, or bulging
- Freezing
- Sudden and accidental damage from artificially generated electrical current
- Volcanic eruption

4-6. Windstorm is not an excluded peril under Coverage A, so coverage would be provided for the exterior and interior damage to Julie's home. Windstorm is a named peril under Coverage C, so coverage would be provided for the damage to Julie's sofa and coffee table. Because wind (a specified peril) caused the branch to damage the structure, leaving an opening that allowed the rain into the home, the water damage to the dining room table would be covered under Coverage C.

4-7. Because no applicable exclusion exists under Coverage A, the losses to Julie's central air conditioner would be covered. Although Coverage C lists the covered peril of sudden and accidental damage from artificially generated electrical current, it makes an exception for losses to computers and home entertainment equipment. Therefore, the Coverage C losses resulting from the power surge would not be covered.

Educational Objective 5

5-1. The Insurable Interest and Limit of Liability condition limits the maximum payment for any single loss to the applicable limits shown on the Declarations page, regardless of the number of insureds who have an insurable interest in the property.

5-2. The purpose of the 2011 revision to the HO-3's Deductible condition was to reinforce the policy's intent that the deductible applies only to Section I losses.

5-3. Examples of the duties the insured must perform after a property loss under the HO-3 include these:

- Give prompt notice

- Notify the police

- Notify the credit card, electronic fund transfer card company, or access device company

- Protect the property from further damage

- Cooperate with the insurer

- Prepare an inventory

- Verify the loss

- Sign a sworn proof of loss

5-4. The Loss Settlement condition establishes the process for determining the amount to be paid for a property loss.

5-5. This is the procedure the HO-3's Appraisal condition outlines for resolving disputes between an insured and the insurer over the amount of a loss:

- The insurer and the insured each choose an appraiser to prepare an estimate of the value of the loss. Each party pays for its own appraiser.

- If the estimates differ, the two appraisers submit their differences to an umpire. The umpire is an impartial individual (often another appraiser or a judge) who resolves the differences. An agreement by any two of the three will set the amount of loss. The insurer and the insured share the cost of the umpire.

5-6. If two or more insurance policies cover the same loss, the HO-3's Other Insurance and Service Agreement condition states that the loss will be shared proportionally by all policies.

5-7. The HO-3's Our Option condition reserves the right for the insurer to repair or replace damaged property with similar property, should it choose to do so.

5-8. The mortgagee rights the Mortgage Clause condition of the HO-3 establishes are these:

- If a loss occurs to property covered by Coverage A—Dwelling or Coverage B—Other Structures, the loss is payable jointly to the mortgagee and the insured.

- A mortgagee has rights that are independent of the insured's rights. If the insurer denies the insured's loss, the mortgagee retains the right to collect from the insurer its insurable interest in the property.

- An insurer must mail notice of cancellation or nonrenewal of a policy to the mortgagee (in addition to notice sent to the insured) at least ten days before the cancellation or nonrenewal.

5-9. The insurer that issued Kim's policy will pay 40 percent of the loss ($100,000 ÷ 250,000), or $80,000 (.40 × $200,000). The insurer that issued Dan's policy will pay 60 percent of the loss ($150,000 ÷ $250,000), or $120,000 (.60 × $200,000).

Educational Objective 6

6-1.   These answers are based on the facts associated with Steve and Kelly's fire case.

a.   The component of the HO-3 policy that would be used to determine whether coverage would apply for Steve and Kelly at the time of the loss is the Declarations page, which specifies the named insured, the address of the covered property, and the period during which coverage applies.

b.   The component of the HO-3 policy that would be used to determine whether the policy applies to Steve and Kelly's loss is the Insuring Agreement, in which the insurer agrees to pay for direct physical loss to property described in Coverages A and B (subject to certain exclusions) and for direct physical loss under Coverage C for certain named perils, including fire and subsequent smoke and water damage.

c.   The $200 special limit of liability for cash would affect the amount that Steve and Kelly receive from the insurer for the money in the cookie jar that was destroyed in the fire. Instead of receiving payment for the $375 that was lost, Steve and Kelly would instead receive $200, the maximum amount allowable according to this policy condition.

d.   Under Coverage A, Steve and Kelly will receive $74,500 ($75,000 less the $500 deductible) for fire damage to the home (within the $300,000 Coverage A limit) at full replacement cost, because the policy dwelling limit complies with policy replacement cost provisions.

e.   Compensation for the television would be settled under Coverage C under the lesser of the television's actual cash value (ACV) at the time of the loss or the amount required to repair the television. The television's ACV can be determined by identifying what it would cost new and then subtracting a percentage of that value based on depreciation. Because the television has consumed half of its useful life, it has depreciated 50 percent. Its ACV, then, would be 50 percent of $600 ($300). Because this amount is less than the $400 it would cost to repair the damage, the claims representative would settle the loss amount for the television at $300.

Direct Your Learning

Homeowners Liability, Conditions, Coverage Forms, and Endorsements

Educational Objectives

After learning the content of this assignment, you should be able to:

1. Determine whether the 2011 Homeowners 3—Special Form (HO-3) policy provisions in the following Section II—Liability Coverages provide coverage for a given loss or loss exposure:

   - Coverage E—Personal Liability

   - Coverage F—Medical Payments to Others

   - Additional Coverages

2. Determine whether one or more exclusions preclude the coverage provided by Section II of the 2011 Homeowners 3—Special Form (HO-3) policy provisions in Section II—Exclusions.

3. Summarize each of these 2011 Homeowners 3—Special Form (HO-3) policy provisions:

   - Conditions applicable to Section II

   - Conditions applicable to Sections I and II

4. Given a case describing a homeowners liability claim, determine whether the Homeowners Section II—Liability Coverages would cover the claim and, if so, the amount the insurer would pay for the claim.

5. Compare the coverage provided by each of the following 2011 homeowners forms to the coverage provided by the 2011 Homeowners 3—Special Form (HO-3):

   - HO-2 Broad Form

   - HO-4 Contents Broad Form

   - HO-5 Comprehensive Form

6

- HO-6 Unit-Owners Form
- HO-8 Modified Coverage Form

6. Summarize the coverages provided by various 2011 ISO Homeowners policy endorsements.

7. Given a case describing a homeowners claim, determine whether a 2011 HO-3 policy that may include one or more endorsements would cover the claim and, if so, the amount the insurer would pay for the claim.

Outline

Narrow the focus of what you need to learn. Remember, the Educational Objectives are the foundation of the course, and the exam is based on these Educational Objectives.

▶▶

Outline

For each assignment, you should define or describe each of the Key Words and Phrases and answer each of the Review and Application Questions.

Educational Objective 1

Determine whether the 2011 Homeowners 3—Special Form (HO-3) policy provisions in the following Section II—Liability Coverages provide coverage for a given loss or loss exposure:

- Coverage E—Personal Liability
- Coverage F—Medical Payments to Others
- Additional Coverages

Key Words and Phrases

Third party

Bodily injury

Property damage

Occurrence

Review Questions

1-1. Explain when the insurer's obligation to defend an insured under Homeowners 3—Special Form (HO-3) Section II Coverage E ends.

1-2. Describe the coverage that is provided and the expenses that are paid under HO-3 Section II Coverage F—Medical Payments to Others.

1-3. Describe how Medical Payments to Others coverage differs from bodily injury liability coverage also provided by Section II.

1-4. List the claims expenses that an insurer may pay under Section II—Additional Coverage on the insured's behalf in addition to any judgment or settlement.

1-5. Describe the types of losses that are covered under the Loss Assessment additional coverage of the HO-3 policy.

Application Question

1-6. Dave has an HO-3 policy to insure his home, personal property, and liability. He shares his home with his ten-year-old son, James. For each of these situations, explain whether coverage would be provided under Coverage E—Personal Liability, Coverage F—Medical Payments to Others, or Section II—Additional Coverages (such as Claim Expense, First Aid Expenses, Damage to Property of Others, or Loss Assessment).

   a. The family's one-year-old German shepherd, which often escapes from its enclosure, ran into their neighbor's yard and attacked their neighbor's three-year-old daughter. She suffered serious bite wounds on her face and arms.

   b. James invited his friend Timmy to their home to play catch under Dave's supervision. Timmy tossed the ball straight up, intending to catch it. However, the ball hit Timmy in the face, breaking his glasses and cutting his cheek. Dave used a bandage and an ice pack from his first-aid kit to treat Timmy's injuries and then called Timmy's parents. Timmy's cut required stitches and resulted in $700 in medical expenses.

   c. Dave was required to join a homeowners association when he bought his home. The association owns a clubhouse. A guest at the clubhouse became permanently disabled after he fell down the stairs. The loss settlement for the claim exceeded the liability limit of the association's policy, so each member was assessed $5,000.

d. Dave borrowed his brother's golf cart for a weekend golf tournament. While his friend Sam was riding in the cart, Dave stopped the cart on a hill and jumped out. However, he failed to properly set the parking brake. The cart rolled down the hill hitting a tree, damaging the cart. Sam jumped out of the cart before it hit the tree but hurt his shoulder when he hit the ground. His shoulder required medical attention. His emergency room bill was $300. Sam is only seeking reimbursement of his medical bills.

Educational Objective 2

Determine whether one or more exclusions preclude the coverage provided by Section II of the 2011 Homeowners 3—Special Form (HO-3) policy provisions in Section II—Exclusions.

Key Word or Phrase

Loss assessment

Review Questions

2-1. Describe the first four exclusions of the Homeowners 3—Special Form (HO-3) policy Section II that apply to losses arising from motor vehicles, watercraft, aircraft, and hovercraft.

2-2.   Explain what the HO-3 Section II Motor Vehicle Exclusion is designed to do.

2-3.   Describe the Expected or Intended Injury exclusion that applies to HO-3 Coverages E and F.

2-4.   Describe the three exceptions to the HO-3 Section II Business exclusion that allow for some common rental situations.

2-5.   Describe the two types of written contracts that are exceptions to the HO-3 Section II Coverage E—Personal Liability exclusion, which eliminates coverage for liability assumed under contract or agreement.

Application Question

2-6. Paul and Terri own a home with a four-stall detached garage and insure it under an HO-3 policy. Their eight-year-old daughter, Stacy, lives with them, as does Holly, their twenty-eight-year-old nanny. The couple's state law requires that homeowners provide workers compensation benefits for domestic workers. For each of these situations, explain which of the HO-3 Section ll Exclusions should be considered and whether the exclusions affect the HO-3 coverage.

a. Stacy sold lemonade from a stand along her street one hot afternoon and inadvertently added a harmful liquid to the product. A customer required a trip to the emergency room for treatment immediately after drinking the tainted lemonade.

b. Paul rents a stall of his garage to his neighbor for her private auto for $40 per month during the winter.

c. Terri is an accountant and prepares income taxes for personal clients each year in her spare time. Terri miscalculated some figures on a tax return she prepared for a client. The error was not found until several years later. The client was required to pay penalties and interest to the federal government.

d. While she was off duty, Holly went to a movie downtown with a friend. After crossing the street by the theater, Holly tripped on the curb and sprained her ankle.

Educational Objective 3

Summarize each of these 2011 Homeowners 3—Special Form (HO-3) policy provisions:

- **Conditions applicable to Section II**
- **Conditions applicable to Sections I and II**

Key Words and Phrases

Severability of Insurance condition

Waiver

Apparent authority

Binding authority

Review Questions

3-1. As described in the Homeowners 3—Special Form (HO-3) Section II Limit of Liability condition, explain how the limits of Coverage E—Personal Liability and of Coverage F—Medical Payments to Others on the Declarations page apply when numerous people are injured in the same occurrence.

3-2. Explain the operation of the Severability of Insurance condition under Section II of the HO-3 in conjunction with the limit of liability.

3-3. Under the HO-3 Section II—Conditions, what are the insured's duties after an occurrence?

3-4. Describe the Payment of Claim condition under HO-3 Coverage F.

3-5. Explain how the HO-3 Section II Concealment or Fraud condition would apply to an insured who was not involved in the concealment or fraud.

3-6. Explain why courts have permitted use of oral waivers by claims representatives made during the adjustment of a loss and after issuance of the written policy.

Application Questions

3-7. Anthony has an HO-3 policy to insure his home, personal property, and liability. He shares his home with his aunt Mabel, who is an insured under the policy. For each of these situations, explain any applicable conditions and how the coverage would be affected.

   a. Mabel's dog escaped one afternoon and entered a nearby grocery store, where he was inadvertently shut in a cooler. The dog destroyed several cases of frozen meat and other goods and damaged the shelving before the grocery staff found him. Mabel retrieved her dog, and the grocery store filed a suit against Mabel and Anthony, individually, for $8,000 each in damages for the loss of product and the loss of use of the cooler. When the legal documents arrived, Mabel notified the insurer of the claim circumstances and forwarded her documents to the insurer, but Anthony failed to forward his legal documents. The grocery store won the suit against Mabel and Anthony. The court found Mabel liable for $8,000 in damages and Anthony liable for $8,000.

b. Anthony invited a friend, Trisha, into his home. Trisha tripped over Mabel's dog, fell through a glass patio door, and required medical treatment that cost $850. Anthony gave written notice to his insurer of the occurrence the following morning. The insurer offered to pay Trisha's medical expenses under Coverage F—Medical Payments to Others.

c. An elderly friend of Mabel's, Esther, tripped on a loose board and fell down the front steps of Anthony's home. Esther broke her hip and was hospitalized for four months, incurring medical expenses of $9,000. Anthony gave written notice to his insurer of the occurrence the following day. Before Esther's treatment was completed, Anthony filed for bankruptcy. The insurer offered to pay $1,000 of Esther's medical expenses under Coverage F—Medical Payments to Others.

3-8. One month after renewing their homeowners insurance policy, Charlotte and Allan sold their home to another couple, Laura and Luke, who had relocated from another state. To make life a little easier for Laura and Luke, Charlotte and Allan decided to transfer their homeowners insurance to them. Explain whether the transfer is legally enforceable.

Educational Objective 4

Given a case describing a homeowners liability claim, determine whether the Homeowners Section II—Liability Coverages would cover the claim and, if so, the amount the insurer would pay for the claim.

Application Question

4-1. Tom and Sandy have an Insurance Services Office, Inc. (ISO) Homeowners 3—Special Form (HO-3) policy covering their home. The policy has Section II Coverage E—Personal Liability with a limit of $500,000 for each occurrence and Coverage F—Medical Payments to Others with a limit of $5,000 for each person. Both Tom and Sandy are listed as named insureds on the policy, and the annual policy has been in effect for six months. Their five-year-old son, Johnny, resides with them. Recently, Sandy's friend Cathy came over to the residence for a card game. Cathy tripped over one of Johnny's toys and suffered a compound fracture in one of her legs, requiring emergency surgery. As a result of her injury, she incurred $20,000 in medical expenses. Moreover, she was unable to work for four months and incurred $30,000 in lost wages. Cathy has made a claim against Tom and Sandy alleging that they are legally liable to pay the damages resulting from the injury she sustained in their home. Tom and Sandy promptly reported the accident to their insurer and are cooperating in the insurer's investigation. Assuming that Tom and Sandy are legally liable for Cathy's damages, will Tom and Sandy's HO-3 cover Cathy's claim? If so, what amount will the insurer pay for the claim? When determining whether coverage applies to the losses, you can apply the four steps of the DICE method. ("DICE" stands for declarations, insuring agreement, conditions, and exclusions.)

a. The first DICE step is to review the policy's declarations page to determine whether the individuals are covered, the location is covered, and the incident occurred during the policy period.

b. The second DICE step is to determine whether the event triggers coverage under an insuring agreement in Section II of the HO-3 policy.

c. The third DICE step is to determine whether all policy conditions have been met.

d. The fourth DICE step is to determine whether one or more exclusions preclude coverage that the insuring agreements have granted.

e. Now that you have completed the DICE analysis, you can determine the amounts payable.

Educational Objective 5

Compare the coverage provided by each of the following 2011 homeowners forms to the coverage provided by the 2011 Homeowners 3—Special Form (HO-3):

- **HO-2 Broad Form**
- **HO-4 Contents Broad Form**
- **HO-5 Comprehensive Form**
- **HO-6 Unit-Owners Form**
- **HO-8 Modified Coverage Form**

Key Words and Phrases

Condominium

Cooperative corporation

Review Questions

5-1. Describe four different situations that the Insurance Services Office, Inc. (ISO) homeowners forms other than the HO-3 are meant to address.

5-2. Where are the primary differences between the HO-3 policy form and the other homeowners forms found?

5-3. Both the HO-2 and HO-3 policy forms are designed for owner-occupants of a house. Why would a homeowner most likely choose to use the HO-2 policy form instead of the HO-3?

5-4. Explain how the burden of proof relating to losses under named perils coverage differs from the burden of proof relating to losses under special form coverage.

5-5. Explain the coverage need that the HO-4 is specifically designed to fill.

5-6. Describe what information about insurance is usually contained in a condominium ownership deed.

Application Questions

5-7. Janet bought a condominium. The condominium declaration or master deed for her condominium association requires the association to purchase insurance to cover only the "bare walls," which applies only to the building structure and walls that support the structure. Janet bought an HO-6 policy to cover her unit, personal property, and liability. After her purchase but before she moved in with her belongings, an electrical fire damaged exterior walls, light fixtures, plumbing fixtures, wiring, and a partition in her unit. Repair estimates indicate that it will cost $2,000 to repair the damage to the exterior walls and that fixing the remaining damage will cost $4,000. It will take one month to complete the repairs, during which time the unit will be uninhabitable. Which coverages from Janet's HO-6 policy may apply to her loss? Explain.

5-8. Jim and Ann purchased an older home located in the old section of their town for a low price. The home has many unique features, including carved wood doors, a spiral staircase, and antique light fixtures that would be expensive to replace if the home sustained major damage. Which homeowners policy would be appropriate for the loss exposures for this home? Explain.

Educational Objective 6

Summarize the coverages provided by various 2011 ISO Homeowners policy endorsements.

Key Word or Phrase

Scheduled coverage

Review Questions

6-1. Explain why many insurers require a higher-than-usual limit for Coverage C—Personal Property when the Personal Property Replacement Cost Loss Settlement endorsement is added to a homeowners policy.

6-2. Explain how the homeowners policy Inflation Guard endorsement operates.

6-3. Explain how the amount of the deductible for the coverage provided by the Earthquake endorsement is determined.

6-4. Describe the commercial coverages that the Home Business Insurance Coverage endorsement provides for eligible businesses.

6-5. Describe what coverage is extended by the Additional Residence Rented to Others—1, 2, 3, or 4 Families endorsement.

Application Questions

6-6. Paul and Deb recently bought a new home, which they insured under an HO-3 policy. The home is located in an area where property values are expected to increase steadily over the next few years. Paul and Deb collect antiques, and Paul owns a coin collection that includes several rare coins. Identify endorsements that Paul and Deb might decide to purchase to modify their HO-3 policy.

6-7. Susan recently started a craft business in the spare bedroom of her home, where she makes decorative wall coverings to sell at local arts and craft shows. She hired her sister to help her make the craft items. Susan insured her house, personal property, and liability with an HO-3 policy. Her insurance agent just learned of her new business. Is there an endorsement he should recommend to Susan?

Educational Objective 7

Given a case describing a homeowners claim, determine whether a 2011 HO-3 policy that may include one or more endorsements would cover the claim and, if so, the amount the insurer would pay for the claim.

Application Question

7-1. Larry and Sarah have an HO-3 policy covering their single family dwelling, which is their primary residence. The policy has Section l Coverage A—Dwelling for $200,000 and Section l Coverage C—Personal Property for $140,000. The coverage for personal property is modified by the Personal Property Replacement Cost Loss Settlement endorsement (HO 04 90). Further, the policy has Section ll Coverage E—Personal Liability for $300,000 for each occurrence that is modified by the Personal Injury Coverage endorsement (HO 24 82).

Both Larry and Sarah are listed as named insureds on the annual policy, which has been in effect for eleven months. Larry was employed in the construction industry. A severe windstorm ripped siding and shingles off his and Sarah's house, and rain water entered the house. It cost $20,000 to remove the debris from and repair the water damage to their dwelling. It also cost $10,000 to repair or replace the water damage to their personal property.

After the storm, Larry's co-worker, George, offered to help with repairs. Larry and Sarah accepted George's help and left him to start work on the job while they went to a home improvement store for supplies. Having heard Larry and Sarah discuss tearing down an interior wall to create more of an open floor plan, George felt that since the house was already in a state of disrepair he should tear down the wall. Unfortunately, his action caused structural damage to the house: It cost $16,000 to remove the debris and repair the resulting damage. Several weeks later, Larry mentioned to his and George's supervisor that George was not competent performing residential construction work. Shortly afterward, the supervisor restricted George's responsibilities to non-construction-related duties and reduced his work hours. George sued Larry for slander, claiming damage to his reputation and lost wages. Larry promptly notified the insurer of the lawsuit.

Given the facts presented in the case, will the homeowners claims be covered? If so, what amount will the insurer pay for each claim? When determining whether coverage applies to the losses, you can apply the four steps of the DICE method.

a. The first DICE step is to review the policy's declarations page to determine whether the individuals are covered, the location is covered, and the incidents occurred during the policy period.

b. The second DICE step is to review the insuring agreement to determine whether it is applicable to the described loss.

c. The third DICE step is to determine whether the policy conditions preclude coverage at the time of loss.

d. The fourth DICE step is to determine whether one or more exclusions exclude or limit coverage of the loss.

e. Now that you have completed the DICE analysis, you can determine the amounts payable.

Answers to Assignment 6 Questions

NOTE: These answers are provided to give students a basic understanding of acceptable types of responses. They often are not the only valid answers and are not intended to provide an exhaustive response to the questions.

Educational Objective 1

1-1. The insurer's obligation to defend ends only when the liability limit for the occurrence is exhausted by payment of a settlement or judgment (even if policy limits are exhausted by the costs of the claim).

1-2. Coverage F—Medical Payments to Others covers medical payments incurred by others (not insureds or regular household residents) under certain conditions within three years of an injury. These medical expenses include reasonable charges for medical, surgical, x-ray, dental, ambulance, hospital, professional nursing, and funeral services, and prosthetic devices. This limit is generally set at $1,000 per person for a single accident.

1-3. Medical Payments to Others coverage may be considered to overlap with bodily injury liability coverage. However, liability coverage applies only when an insured is legally responsible for damages. Claims for medical payments are often paid when the insured feels a moral obligation to another person, even though the insured is not negligent or legally responsible. When a bodily injury claim involves a relatively small amount of money, paying it as a Medical Payments to Others claim simplifies matters by eliminating any need to determine whether an insured was legally responsible for the injuries.

1-4. These Additional Coverage expenses may be paid on the insured's behalf:

- Expenses the insurer incurs

- Premiums on bonds

- Reasonable expenses

- Postjudgment interest

1-5. The Loss Assessment additional coverage provides up to $1,000 for an insured's share of a loss assessment charged to the insured by a corporation or an association of property owners for these types of losses:

- Bodily injury or property damage that is not excluded under Section II of the homeowners policy

- Liability that results from an act of an elected and unpaid director, officer, or trustee

1-6. These answers address questions regarding Dave's HO-3 case study:

a. Coverage F will provide $1,000 medical payments coverage for the girl's injuries. Coverage E will provide liability coverage for the girl's injuries and damages, assuming Dave is legally liable. If the neighbors sue Dave, Coverage E will pay his defense costs until the liability limit for the occurrence is exhausted by payment of a settlement or judgment. Section II—Additional Coverages will cover certain claims expenses related to any lawsuit that ensued in addition to any settlement or judgment.

b. Coverage F will pay the $700 in medical expenses because Timmy was an invited guest and the injury was accidental. Because Timmy is responsible for his own injury and Dave was properly supervising the children when the accident occurred, he probably would not be liable for the damages and Coverage E would not be needed. However, Section II—Additional Coverages will reimburse Dave for the first-aid supplies he used. These payments can be made without litigation and the need to determine fault.

c. The Loss Assessment provision under Section II—Additional Coverages will pay $1,000 for Dave's share of the loss assessment.

d. Coverage E will pay for the property damage to Dave's brother's cart. Coverage F will pay up to $1,000 for Sam's medical expenses. Coverage E is also available for Sam's bodily injury loss, if needed.

Educational Objective 2

2-1. These are the first four exclusions of HO-3 Section II that apply to losses arising from motor vehicles, watercraft, aircraft, and hovercraft:

- The ownership, maintenance, occupancy, operation, use, loading, or unloading of a motor vehicle or craft by any person unless it appears in a specific exception to the exclusion

- Negligent entrustment, by an insured, of an excluded motor vehicle or craft

- An insured's failure to supervise, or negligence in supervising, a person

- An insured's "vicarious liability" for the actions of a child or minor

2-2. The HO-3 Section II Motor Vehicle Liability exclusion is designed to limit the majority of personal motor vehicle loss exposures that would typically be insured under a Personal Auto Policy (PAP).

2-3. The HO-3 Section II Expected or Intended Injury exclusion applies to any bodily injury or property damage caused by an insured when the bodily injury or property damage is intentional or expected, even if the actual injury or damage resulting from the action was unintended when the intentional action took place.

2-4. These are the three exceptions to the HO-3 Section II Business exclusion that allow for some common rental situations:

- Rental of an insured location on an occasional basis is a covered loss exposure if the location is used only as a residence.

- Rental of part of an insured location as a residence is a covered loss exposure, as long as the occupying family takes no more than two roomers or boarders in a single-family unit.

- Rental of part of an insured location is a covered loss exposure if it is used only as an office or a school, studio, or private garage.

2-5. The two types of written contracts that are exceptions to the HO-3 Section II Coverage E—Personal Liability exclusion, which eliminates coverage for liability assumed under contract or agreement, are these:

- Contracts relating to the ownership, maintenance, or use of an insured location

- Contracts relating to the liability of others assumed by the named insured before an accident occurs

2-6. These answers address questions regarding the HO-3 Exclusions case study:

a. The Coverage E and F Business exclusion could be considered. However, the Business exclusion is designed to exclude coverage for bodily injury or property damage arising out of business activities of an insured while providing coverage for occasional or part-time activities, such as insureds under the age of twenty-one selling lemonade. Another exception involves activities for which the insured receives $2,000 or less during the year preceding the policy period, which likely applies to Stacy's lemonade stand operations. So liability coverage applies.

b. The Coverage E and F Business exclusion could be considered. However, liability for rental as a private garage is an exception to the exclusion. So coverage is provided.

c. The Coverage E and F Professional Services exclusion could be considered. The exclusion would apply to Terri's tax preparation business, for which her liability should be covered under a professional liability policy. Therefore, no coverage applies under the HO-3 policy.

d. The Coverage F Residence Employee Off Premises exclusion and the Coverage E Bodily Injury to Persons Eligible for Workers Compensation Benefits exclusion should be considered. The Residence Employee Off Premises—Coverage F excludes bodily injury to a residence employee if the injury occurs off the insured's location and the injury does not arise out of the employee's work. Holly was off the insured's location and off duty at the time of the injury, so the exclusion applies. In addition, the Bodily Injury to Persons Eligible for Workers Compensation Benefits—Coverage E excludes coverage for Holly for her bodily injury because she is eligible to receive benefits as an insured under her state's workers compensation law. So no coverage applies under the HO-3 policy.

Educational Objective 3

3-1. The Section II Limit of Liability provision stipulates that the limit of Coverage E—Personal Liability appearing on the Declarations page is the total limit of coverage for any one occurrence. This limit does not increase, regardless of the number of insureds, claims made, or people injured. This condition further states that the limit of liability applicable to Coverage F—Medical Payments to Others for all medical expenses for bodily injury to one person as the result of an accident cannot exceed the Coverage F limit shown on the Declarations page. The Coverage F limit can apply to more than one person per accident.

3-2. Under the Severability of Insurance condition, each insured seeking protection is treated as if he or she has separate coverage under the policy. However, the insurer's limit of liability stated in the policy is not increased for any one occurrence if more than one insured is involved.

3-3. The insured's duties after an occurrence include these requirements:

- Give written notice to the insurer as soon as practical.

- Cooperate with the insurer's investigation, settlement, and defense activities.

- Forward legal documents promptly to the insurer.

- Provide claims assistance to the insurer in making a settlement, enforcing any right of contribution against another party, attending hearings and trials, securing and giving evidence, and obtaining the attendance of witnesses.

- Submit evidence for damage to property of others when a claim is made under the additional coverage for damage to property of others; the insured must submit to the insurer a sworn statement of loss and show the damaged property to the insurer.

- Do not make voluntary payment; if the insured does so, it will be at the insured's own expense.

3-4. The Coverage F Payment of Claim condition stipulates that the insurer's payment of a Medical Payments to Others claim is not an admission of liability by the insured or the insurer. The intent of Section II medical payments coverage is to prevent suits or to reduce the damages resulting from possible claims by providing prompt payment for injured parties' medical expenses without the need to determine fault.

3-5. The Concealment or Fraud condition excludes coverage only for the insured(s) involved in the concealment or fraud, or those making false statements. Other innocent insureds would not be excluded from liability coverage.

3-6. Courts have permitted use of oral waivers by claims representatives made during the adjustment of a loss and after the written policy was issued because claims representatives are the insurer's representatives and have apparent authority to modify policy conditions.

3-7. These answers address questions regarding the Anthony and Mabel case study:

a. Two conditions could affect coverage under Section II Coverage E of Anthony's policy—the Duties After "Occurrence" and the Severability of Insurance conditions. Because Mabel is an insured, coverage is provided under the policy for her liability. Mabel complied with the conditions specified for Duties After "Occurrence," so coverage would be provided for Mabel's liability of $8,000 up to the policy limits. But Anthony did not comply with the duties, which hindered the insurer in performing its duties. Consequently, the insurer is not obligated to pay Anthony's liability under the policy. The Severability of Insurance condition allows Mabel to be treated as if she has separate coverage under the policy, so the insurer's denial of payment for Anthony's liability would not affect its payment of Mabel's liability. Anthony could be held personally responsible for the $8,000 liability settlement against him. Finally, the Suit Against Us condition could bar Anthony from suing his insurer for failure to pay the judgment because he did not meet all of his obligations under Section II of the policy.

b. To obtain medical payments coverage, Trisha must comply with all requirements under the Duties of an Injured Person condition of Coverage F. The Payment of Claim condition also applies here, stipulating that the insurer's payment of Trisha's Medical Payments to Others claim is not an admission of liability for the occurrence. Anthony complied with the Duties After "Occurrence" condition, so coverage was provided.

▶▶

    c.   Because Anthony complied with the Duties After "Occurrence" condition, coverage was available under the policy. To obtain Medical Payments coverage, Esther must comply with the Duties of an Injured Person condition of Coverage F, and the Payment of Claim condition would specify that the payment was not an admission of liability. Even though Anthony filed bankruptcy, the Bankruptcy of an Insured condition still obligated the insurer to pay Esther's bodily injury claim under Coverage E—Personal Liability.

3-8.   Charlotte and Allan's transfer of their homeowners policy to Laura and Luke may not be legally enforceable, because an insurance policy is a personal contract between the insurer and the policyholder. Therefore, the insurer is able to choose whom it will insure. The assignment condition states that any assignment of the policy will not be valid unless the insurer provides its written consent.

Educational Objective 4

4-1.   These answers relate to the Tom and Sandy case:

    a.   In this case, the policy lists Tom and Sandy as named insureds, and the accident occurred at their residence during the policy period.

    b.   Cathy's liability claim against Tom and Sandy triggers coverage under the Coverage E—Personal Liability insuring agreement because her claim alleges damages because of bodily injury for which Tom and Sandy are legally liable. Cathy's broken leg qualifies as bodily injury and Tom and Sandy both meet the policy definition of insured. Cathy's medical expenses (but not her loss of wages or pain and suffering) could also be covered under the Coverage F—Medical Payments to Others insurance agreement (up to the $5,000 limit). However, because Cathy has made a liability claim against Tom and Sandy, the claim will be handled under the Coverage E insuring agreement only.

    c.   The relevant policy conditions include promptly notifying the insurer of the loss and assisting the insurer as requested in its investigation. Tom and Sandy have fulfilled both of these conditions.

    d.   Based on the case facts, no exclusions apply to this accident.

    e.   The insurer will pay Cathy's medical expenses ($20,000), her lost wages ($30,000), and whatever sum is either negotiated in a settlement with the insurer or awarded by a court for her pain and suffering. If Cathy's pain and suffering is determined to be $5,000, the insurer would pay a total of $55,000 in damages, which is less than the Coverage E limit. Any costs incurred to defend Tom and Sandy against Cathy's suit would be payable in full, not subject to the limit of insurance.

Educational Objective 5

5-1. Four different situations that the ISO homeowners forms other than the HO-3 are meant to address include these:

- Apartment dwellers and condominium unit owners do not need full insurance on the buildings in which they live.

- Some customers will accept more restricted coverage than the HO-3 provides in exchange for lower premiums.

- Some customers are willing to pay for the broadest coverage possible.

- Some older homes that have depreciated substantially are not well suited for the replacement cost coverage provided by the HO-3.

5-2. The primary differences between the HO-3 policy form and the other homeowners forms are in each form's Section I—Property Coverages. The remaining sections of the coverage forms are very similar. The Agreement, Section II—Liability Coverages, and Section II—Conditions are identical in all the standard, unendorsed ISO homeowners forms.

5-3. A homeowner might choose to use the HO-2 policy form instead of the HO-3 because the HO-2 covers the dwelling and other structures against fewer causes of loss. In the HO-2, covered causes of loss are limited to the named perils listed in the policy, not only for personal property but also for the building and other structures. Therefore, it has a slightly lower premium than an HO-3 with similar limits.

5-4. With named perils coverage, such as the HO-2, the insured must prove that the loss was caused by a covered cause of loss for coverage to apply. The burden of proof is on the insured. With special form coverage (such as Coverages A and B of the HO-3), if a loss to covered property occurs, the initial assumption is that it is covered. To deny coverage, the insurer must prove that the loss was caused by an excluded cause of loss. The burden of proof in this case is on the insurer.

5-5. The HO-4 is designed specifically for the needs of persons who live in rented houses or apartments.

5-6. A condominium ownership deed (called a condominium declaration or a master deed) usually contains insurance requirements and describes the insurance provided for the jointly owned property (called condominium association insurance, or a condominium master policy). Property not covered by this insurance is usually the individual unit owner's responsibility.

5-7. Coverage A Dwelling of Janet's HO-6 policy provides a basic limit of $5,000. The repair bill of $4,000 is payable by her insurer. The $2,000 to repair the exterior walls should be covered by the condominium association insurance. Also, because Janet had not yet moved in her personal property, it is likely that Coverage C Personal Property of her policy will also not be needed. However, Coverage D Loss of Use should be helpful. Janet's unit will be uninhabitable until the repairs are complete, which is estimated to take one month. During that time, Janet will have to find another place to live. Coverage D will pay the cost to rent this other place. Coverage D is limited to 50 percent of Coverage C.

5-8.   An HO-8 policy would be a logical choice for Jim and Ann because replacement of the unique features due to a covered cause of loss would likely exceed the market value of the house. When the market value is substantially lower than the replacement cost, the situation creates an obvious moral hazard, and Jim and Ann's insurer may be unwilling to cover them with any other form. The HO-8 addresses this potential problem under Section I—Conditions. A provision in this section specifies that if the insured makes repairs after a loss, the insurer will not pay more than the cost of "common construction materials and methods" that are "functionally equivalent to and less costly than obsolete, antique, or custom construction."

Educational Objective 6

6-1.   The value of personal property based on replacement cost is usually higher than the value of personal property based on actual cash value. Accordingly, when the Personal Property Replacement Cost Loss Settlement endorsement is used, many insurers require a Coverage C—Personal Property limit that is higher than the usual Coverage C limit of 50 percent of the Coverage A limit (used with actual cash value coverage).

6-2.   Rather than increasing coverage by a fixed amount, the Inflation Guard endorsement gradually and automatically increases limits for Coverages A, B, C, and D throughout the policy period by a percentage mutually agreed upon by the insured and insurer.

6-3.   The mandatory deductible for the coverage provided by the Earthquake endorsement is usually 5 percent of the limit that applies to either Coverage A or Coverage C, whichever is greater, but not less than $500.

6-4.   For eligible businesses, the Home Business Insurance Coverage endorsement provides valuable commercial coverages:

- Section I—Property Coverage provides full Coverage C—Personal Property limits for business property, accounts receivable, loss of business income, extra expense, and increased Coverage C limits for other property.

- Section II—Liability Coverages provides products-completed operations coverage up to an annual aggregate limit equal to the Coverage E—Personal Liability limit; provides all other business liability coverage (including personal and advertising injury).

6-5.   The Additional Residence Rented to Others—1, 2, 3, or 4 Families endorsement extends Coverage E—Personal Liability and Coverage F—Medical Payments to Others to one- to four-family residences that are owned by the insured and rented to others.

6-6.   Paul and Deb might choose to purchase these endorsements to modify their HO-3 policy:

- Inflation Guard endorsement to automatically increase coverage limits as the property values increase in the area

- Scheduled Personal Property endorsement to provide coverage for their antiques and coin collection

6-7. For insureds who operate an office or business from their homes, the Home Business Insurance Coverage, or HOMEBIZ, endorsement provides a comprehensive business package policy when attached to a homeowners form. There are minimum requirements for a home business to be covered under this endorsement, such as ownership by an insured, operation from the residence premises, and a maximum of three employees. Susan meets those minimum requirements and is eligible for the additional coverages provided by the endorsement for Section I—Property Coverage and Section II—Liability Coverages.

Educational Objective 7

7-1. These answers address questions regarding the case study about Larry, Sarah, and George.

a. In this case, Larry and Sarah are the named insureds, and they are covered. The loss occurred on the residence premises, which is a covered location. The water damage and allegedly slanderous remark by Larry occurred during the policy period.

b. Section l—Property Coverages A and C contain an insuring agreement that covers the windstorm loss, including debris removal. The damage caused by George's removal of a wall is not covered because his remodeling attempts are likely not a covered peril. The slanderous remark made by Larry is triggered by the insuring agreement, as modified by the Personal Injury Coverage endorsement.

c. Larry and Sarah complied with all the policy conditions regarding the windstorm loss and slander claim by George. They reported the loss and claim in a timely manner and cooperated in the insurer's investigation of the loss and claim.

d. The homeowners insurer could assert that Larry and Sarah were negligent in not supervising George's repair efforts after the water damage occurred. Further, the damage George caused by tearing down the wall is likely not covered.

e. The cost of $20,000 to remove the debris and repair the water damage to the house is within the limit of $200,000 of Section l Coverage A—Dwelling and should be paid in full minus the deductible. The cost of $10,000 to repair or replace the water damage to Larry and Sarah's personal property is within the limit of $140,000 of Section l—Personal Property and should also be paid in full with no deduction for depreciation because of the Personal Property Replacement Cost Loss Settlement endorsement. The cost of $16,000 to remove the debris and repair the damage caused by George's wall removal is likely not covered because it is not caused by a covered peril. The cost to defend and pay a settlement or judgment amount from George's slander suit against Larry claiming damage to his reputation and lost wages is likely covered up to the Section ll Coverage E—Personal Liability limit of $300,000 because of the Personal Injury Coverage endorsement.

Direct Your Learning

Other Residential Insurance

Educational Objectives

After learning the content of this assignment, you should be able to:

1. Contrast the DP-3 policy with the HO-3 policy in regard to each of the following:

   - Types of property covered

   - Other coverages

   - Perils insured against

   - Exclusions and conditions

   - Coverage for liability and theft losses

2. Given a case describing a dwelling claim, determine whether the Dwelling Property—Special Form (DP-3) policy would cover the claim and, if so, the amount the insurer would pay for the claim.

3. Explain how the coverages under the HO-3 policy are modified by the Mobilehome Endorsement (MH 04 01) and other ISO endorsements unique to mobilehome coverage.

4. Describe the operation of the National Flood Insurance Program and the coverage it provides.

5. Describe the operation of FAIR plans and beachfront and windstorm plans and the coverage they provide.

Outline

▶ **Dwelling Policies**
  A. Structures Eligible for Dwelling Policies
  B. Coverages
    1. Coverage A—Dwelling
    2. Coverage B—Other Structures
    3. Coverage C—Personal Property
    4. Coverage D—Fair Rental Value and Coverage E—Additional Living Expense
  C. Other Coverages
    1. Other Structures
    2. Debris Removal
    3. Improvements, Alterations, and Additions
    4. Worldwide Coverage
    5. Fair Rental Value and Additional Living Expense
    6. Reasonable Repairs
    7. Property Removed
    8. Trees, Shrubs, and Other Plants
    9. Fire Department Service Charge
    10. Collapse
    11. Glass or Safety Glazing Material
    12. Ordinance or Law
  D. Perils Insured Against
    1. Coverage A—Dwelling and Coverage B—Other Structures
    2. Coverage C—Personal Property
  E. Dwelling Policy General Exclusions
  F. Dwelling Policy Conditions
  G. Coverage for Liability and Theft Losses
    1. Personal Liability Supplement
    2. Residential Theft Coverage
▶ **Dwelling Coverage Case Study**
  A. Case Facts
  B. Case Analysis Tools
  C. Determination of Coverage
  D. Determination of Amounts Payable

▶ **Mobilehome Coverage**
  A. Mobilehome Exposures
    1. Vulnerability to Additional Exposures
    2. Other Property Exposure Considerations
  B. Mobilehome Coverages
▶ **The National Flood Insurance Program**
  A. Community Eligibility
  B. Incentives and Programs
    1. Emergency Program
    2. Regular Program
  C. Flood Insurance Coverage
    1. Waiting Period
    2. Write-Your-Own (WYO) Program
  D. Flood Insurance Reform
▶ **FAIR and Beachfront and Windstorm Plans**
  A. FAIR Plans
    1. Purpose and Operation
    2. Eligible Property
    3. Coverages
  B. Beachfront and Windstorm Plans
    1. Purpose and Operation
    2. Eligible Property
    3. Coverages

If you are not sure that you have the current materials for the exam you plan to take, please contact The Institutes.

For each assignment, you should define or describe each of the Key Words and Phrases and answer each of the Review and Application Questions.

Educational Objective 1

Contrast the DP-3 policy with the HO-3 policy in regard to each of the following:

- **Types of property covered**
- **Other coverages**
- **Perils insured against**
- **Exclusions and conditions**
- **Coverage for liability and theft losses**

Review Questions

1-1. Under what circumstances would an applicant purchase a dwelling policy rather than a homeowners policy to insure a residence?

1-2. What is the most important difference between an unendorsed Dwelling Property 3—Special Form (DP-3) policy and a homeowners policy?

1-3. Identify the structures that are eligible for dwelling policies.

1-4. How does the availability of property coverages under the dwelling policy differ from the availability of property coverages under the homeowners policy?

1-5. How does Coverage A—Dwelling coverage under the DP-3 differ from that coverage under the HO-3?

1-6. How are gravemarkers and mausoleums treated differently under the DP-3 Coverage B—Other Structures compared with treatment of such property under the HO-3?

1-7. Under the DP-3, when Coverage C—Personal Property is selected and specified with a limit on the Declarations page, how does the coverage differ from property covered under special limits of liability in Coverage C of the HO-3?

▶▶

1-8. How does Coverage D—Fair Rental Value and Coverage E—Additional Living
      Expenses under the DP-3 compare to comparable coverages under the HO-3?

1-9. Explain how each of these Other Coverages under the DP-3 differ from any
      comparable coverages under the HO-3:

      a.   Other Structures

      b.   Improvements, Alterations, and Additions

      c.   Worldwide Coverage

d. Fair Rental Value and Additional Living Expense

e. Ordinance or Law

1-10. How do the perils insured against under the DP-3 Coverages A and B differ from the perils insured against for those coverages under the HO-3?

1-11. Explain how the general exclusions under the DP-3 compare to the HO-3 Section I exclusions.

1-12. Explain the options for insureds who purchase dwelling policies and wish to add coverage for personal liability.

1-13. Identify the two residential theft endorsements from which an insured may choose to add theft coverage to a dwelling policy, and explain the difference between them.

Application Question

1-14. Sally has a DP-3 policy to insure her rural dwelling and personal property. Limits for Coverages A and C are listed on her Declarations page, and she paid the appropriate premium. She purchased no additional endorsements. For each of these situations, explain whether coverage would be provided and, if so, identify the applicable coverage(s):

   a. Sally's toaster malfunctioned and caused a fire in her kitchen while she was working outside. Before the fire department from the neighboring city could respond, her kitchen and appliances sustained extensive damage from the fire and smoke. Silverware, dishes, $500 cash, and other items of personal property in the kitchen were destroyed. The remainder of the dwelling sustained smoke damage. Sally purchased a large, heavy tarp to cover the damaged area of her roof to avoid further damage to the property. She was forced to rent an apartment until the damage was repaired.

   b. An invited guest to Sally's dwelling tripped on a rug in the hallway and fell, breaking his arm.

c. While Sally was at work, her dwelling was broken into and someone stole her personal computer, her television, $3,000 worth of jewelry, and $1,000 in cash and bank notes.

d. Sally returned from work one day to find her storm door shattered and a hole in the etched-glass window of her front door. She found a rock lying among the glass shards on her living room floor.

e. One afternoon, Sally's sewer backed up while she was doing laundry because of tree roots that had grown into the drain and caused a blockage. Her basement carpet in the adjoining room was damaged by the backup of sewer water.

Educational Objective 2

Given a case describing a dwelling claim, determine whether the Dwelling Property—Special Form (DP-3) policy would cover the claim and, if so, the amount the insurer would pay for the claim.

Application Questions

2-1. Scott and Sue have an Insurance Services Office, Inc. (ISO) Dwelling Property 3—Special Form (DP-3) policy on their home. The home is adjacent to a factory that emits smoke from its smokestacks. While Scott and Sue were away on vacation, they left an upstairs back window open. Atmospheric conditions caused the smoke from the factory to accumulate and linger rather than dissipate. The smoke entered the open window of Scott and Sue's home and damaged drapes and upholstered furniture. Does the couple's policy cover this loss?

2-2. Josh, a single father, owns a home where he lives with his two children, Lisa, age three, and Mia, age eleven. Josh has an ISO DP-3 policy on the home. On May 25, a fire caused extensive smoke damage to the interior of the house and its furnishings; Josh's DP-3 covered the damage. While the home was being repaired, Josh rented an apartment for his family to stay in for $1,200 a month. Because Mia was to spend the entire month of July at camp, Josh enrolled Lisa in a daycare center located near the apartment. Although the house became habitable July 15, Josh and Lisa remained in the apartment until Mia returned on August 1. Explain how Josh's insurer would handle their additional living expenses for that period.

2-3. A house insured by an ISO DP-3 policy was vacant for a month and then was burglarized. The thief broke the framing of a door to get in and damaged several kitchen cabinet drawers while searching for valuables. What is covered?

Educational Objective 3

Explain how the coverages under the HO-3 policy are modified by the Mobilehome Endorsement (MH 04 01) and other ISO endorsements unique to mobilehome coverage.

Review Questions

3-1. Identify three exposures to loss faced by owners of mobile homes that are similar to exposures faced by owners of conventional homes.

3-2. To what additional exposures are mobile homes vulnerable because of their construction? Explain your answer.

3-3. Explain how the use of mobile homes as vacation homes affects their vulnerability to additional exposures.

3-4. Explain why the distinction between the dwelling coverage and personal property coverage is a special consideration for mobile homes.

3-5. Describe each of these modifications to the HO-3 policy that result from adding a Mobilehome Endorsement and a declarations page to create a mobilehome policy.

a. Definition of "residence premises"

b. Coverage A property

   c. "Property removed" coverage

   d. Coverage for repair or replacement of panels

3-6. Describe each of these additional mobilehome endorsements.

   a. Actual Cash Value Mobilehome endorsement

   b. Transportation/Permission to Move endorsement

   c. Mobilehome Lienholder's Single Interest endorsement

d. Broadened Residence Premises Definition endorsement

Application Question

3-7. Jake wants to insure his mobile home with a mobilehome policy. The mobile home, which is permanently anchored in its wooded, secluded location, meets the insurer's requirements for coverage. For the following exposures, what coverage would be provided in the mobilehome policy/endorsement and the additional available endorsements?

a. High winds are common in this area and could threaten the entire structure or the panels on the mobile home. Temporary removal of the mobile home offers Jake an option to avoid or reduce the damage.

b. Jake's lienholder is concerned about its interest in the mobile home above Jake's interests. It is concerned about transportation perils and any ordinances that might alter its right to the mobile home as collateral. In accordance with its business policies, the lienholder requires coverage to protect it from Jake's secretion of the mobile home.

Educational Objective 4

Describe the operation of the National Flood Insurance Program and the coverage it provides.

Key Words and Phrases

Special flood hazard area (SFHA)

Flood hazard boundary map

Emergency program

Flood Insurance Rate Map (FIRM)

Regular program

Write-Your-Own (WYO) program

Review Questions

4-1. Describe the two ways a community's residents become eligible for flood insurance under the National Flood Insurance Program (NFIP).

4-2. Describe the assistance available to special flood hazard area (SFHA) residents not participating in the NFIP if disaster occurs as a result of flooding in a community, and any special restrictions on assistance.

4-3. Describe the insurance that property owners can purchase when a community first joins the NFIP and the actions the FIA takes when a community first joins the NFIP.

4-4. Describe the three federal flood insurance policies available to insureds.

4-5. How long is the waiting period required by the NFIP, and why is it required?

4-6. Describe the exception to the NFIP's waiting period.

4-7. Describe the roles of the FIA, NFIP, and an insurer participating in the Write-Your-Own (WYO) program.

Application Question

4-8. Karen purchased a home for $250,000 in a community that is eligible for flood insurance under the NFIP emergency program. Karen's home is in a special flood hazard area. What incentive does Karen have to encourage her community to enter the NFIP regular program as soon as possible?

Educational Objective 5
Describe the operation of FAIR plans and beachfront and windstorm plans and the coverage they provide.

Key Words and Phrases

Syndicate

Difference in conditions (DIC) policy, or DIC insurance

Review Questions

5-1. What is the purpose of a Fair Access to Insurance Requirements (FAIR) plan (or a beachfront and windstorm plan)?

5-2. Describe three types of loss exposures that resulted in the creation of FAIR plans.

5-3. Explain how FAIR plans provide insurance, service policies, and fund losses paid under the plan.

5-4. If a FAIR plan administrator finds that a property fails to meet the basic safety levels, can the owner obtain coverage under a state FAIR plan? Explain your answer.

5-5. What four coverages are usually available under FAIR plans?

5-6. Describe the various operations of beachfront and windstorm plans.

5-7. What requirements do states have for properties to be eligible for coverage under beachfront and windstorm plans?

5-8. What are the two primary perils insured against under beachfront and wind-storm plans?

5-9. What special provision under beachfront and windstorm plans might restrict applications for new coverage and/or increases in limits?

Application Question

5-10. Sarah wishes to purchase an expensive home in a suburb that is located near a heavily wooded area. Because of the increased fire hazard, she is unable to obtain insurance for the property. The financing organization requires insurance coverage and recommends that Sarah apply for coverage under the state FAIR plan.

   a. What must Sarah do for her otherwise uninsurable property to be eligible under the FAIR plan?

b. Because Sarah's state FAIR plan provides only fire, vandalism, riot, and windstorm coverages, and the financing organization requires coverage against all common homeowners perils, what action should Sarah take to obtain the needed coverage? Explain your answer.

Answers to Assignment 7 Questions

NOTE: These answers are provided to give students a basic understanding of acceptable types of responses. They often are not the only valid answers and are not intended to provide an exhaustive response to the questions.

Educational Objective 1

1-1. An applicant would purchase a dwelling policy rather than a homeowners policy if the residence is not eligible for homeowners coverage because it is not owner-occupied, the dwelling is below the minimum limit for a homeowners policy, or the residence does not otherwise meet an insurer's underwriting guidelines. Also, some insureds do not want or need the full range of homeowners coverages, and a homeowners policy might cost more than the insured is willing to pay.

1-2. The most important difference between an unendorsed DP-3 policy and a homeowners policy is that, unlike most homeowners policies, an unendorsed DP-3 does not provide any theft coverage for personal property or any liability coverages.

1-3. Structures eligible for dwelling policies include these:

- Owner-occupied or tenant-occupied one- to four-family dwellings

- A dwelling in the course of construction

- Mobile homes at a permanent location

- Houseboats, in some states

- Certain incidental business occupancies, if the businesses are operated by the owner-insured or by a tenant of the insured location

1-4. The same property coverages can apply under the dwelling policy that are included under the homeowners policy; however, under the dwelling policy, each desired coverage must be listed with a limit on the Declarations page for the coverage to apply. In contrast, under the homeowners policy, all of these coverages apply automatically.

1-5. The DP-3 form specifies that coverage is provided for the dwelling on the location described in the declarations and specifies that it must be used principally for dwelling purposes. In contrast, the HO-3 refers to the dwelling on the residence premises, including attached structures. The DP-3 also states that coverage is provided for building and outdoor equipment used for the service of the premises and located on the described location, unless it is covered elsewhere in the policy. While the HO-3 covers this property, it is covered under Coverage C—Personal Property.

1-6. Under the DP-3 Coverage B, gravemarkers and mausoleums are specifically excluded. In contrast, the HO-3 Additional Coverage provides up to $5,000 for gravemarkers.

1-7. The HO-3 Coverage C specifies special limits that apply to specific types of personal property. Because the perils and some coverages differ under the DP-3 policy, these limits are not necessary; therefore, no specified limits apply for specific types of property.

▶▶

1-8.   Coverages D and E in the DP-3 form correspond roughly to Coverage D—Loss of Use in the HO-3 form (which essentially provides coverage for both). Coverage D covers the fair rental value of a property rented to others when it becomes unfit for normal use because of a covered loss. Coverage E covers the increase in living expenses when the described property becomes unfit for normal use because of a covered loss.

1-9.   These answers address questions regarding Other Coverages under the DP-3 and how they differ from any comparable coverages under the HO-3.

   a.   Under the Other Coverages provision, the DP-3 form provides up to 10 percent of the Coverage A limit for Coverage B—Other Structures. This additional insurance amount does not reduce the Coverage A limit for the same loss.

   b.   The DP-3 form provides 10 percent of the Coverage C limit as additional insurance to cover a tenant's improvements, alterations, and additions for a covered loss. The HO-3 has no comparable coverage.

   c.   The DP-3 form provides up to 10 percent of the Coverage C limit for loss to the Coverage C property anywhere in the world (as does the HO-3 Coverage C), except that the DP-3 Coverage C excludes rowboats and canoes. Additionally, the HO-3 Coverage C limits the coverage for property that is usually located at a secondary residence of the insured to 10 percent.

   d.   The DP-3 form provides up to 20 percent of the Coverage A limit for losses under both Coverages D and E. In contrast, under the HO-3 form, the corresponding additional limit for loss of use is 30 percent of the Coverage A limit.

   e.   The DP-3 form provides coverage for increased costs the insured incurs because of the enforcement of any ordinance or law. If the insured purchased Coverage A, ordinance or law coverage is 10 percent of the Coverage A limit. If no Coverage A limit exists, then up to 10 percent of the Coverage B limit is provided for ordinance or law coverage. In contrast, the HO-3 form provides up to 10 percent of Coverage A for ordinance and law coverage as an additional coverage. Under the DP-3, if the insured is a tenant, the 10 percent limit applies to improvements, alterations, and additions.

1-10. The DP-3 and the HO-3 approach the perils insured against in the same manner (using a special form approach in which excluded perils are not covered); however, more perils are excluded under the DP-3, such as theft of property that is not part of a covered building or structure and wind, hail, ice, snow, or sleet that damage specific types of property.

1-11. The general exclusions in the DP-3 closely resemble the HO-3 Section I exclusions including loss caused directly or indirectly by several specified perils or events. These perils and events are essentially the same in both policies.

1-12. Insureds who purchase dwelling policies can add a personal liability supplement, either written as an addendum to the dwelling policy or as a separate policy using the personal liability supplement. If an insured has both a homeowners policy on a residence and a dwelling policy on a rental dwelling, then that insured can purchase a homeowners additional residence rented to others endorsement to cover the liability for the rented dwelling.

1-13. The Broad Theft Coverage endorsement provides coverage against the perils of theft, including attempted theft, and vandalism or malicious mischief as a result of theft or attempted theft on-premises and off-premises (available if on-premises coverage is purchased). The endorsement specifies special limits. The Limited Theft Coverage endorsement covers the same perils as the other theft endorsement but applies only on-premises. This endorsement includes special limits only for watercraft and their trailers, trailers not used for watercraft, and firearms and related equipment.

1-14. These answers address questions regarding Sally's DP-3 policy.

a. Sally's property damage to the kitchen and other parts of the dwelling would be covered under her DP-3 policy, Coverage A—Dwelling up to the limits specified in the Declarations page. Except for the $500 cash (money is excluded), her personal property, including the silverware and dishes, would be covered under Coverage C—Personal Property on an actual cash value (ACV) basis up to the limits specified in the Declarations page. The DP-3 other coverage for reasonable repairs would cover the cost of the tarp that Sally purchased and any cost to attach it to the roof (if within the Coverage A limit), and the fire department service charge would be covered up to $500. Because Coverage E—Additional Living Expense is automatically included in the DP-3 policy, Sally has coverage for her rental expense until the damage is repaired.

b. Sally's unendorsed DP-3 policy does not provide any liability coverage. Therefore, no coverage would be provided for the guest's injuries.

c. Sally's unendorsed DP-3 policy does not provide any coverage for personal property theft losses. Therefore, no coverage would be provided for the computer, television, jewelry, cash, or bank notes. However, Coverage A would pay for any damage to the dwelling caused by the burglar.

d. The other coverage glass or safety glazing material under Sally's DP-3 policy would pay to replace the storm door and the glass in the front door.

e. A general exclusion under the DP-3 excludes water damage such as that caused by flood and backup of sewers and drains. Therefore, Sally's DP-3 would provide no coverage for the damaged carpet.

Educational Objective 2

2-1. The damage to Scott and Sue's furniture would not be covered under their DP-3 because smoke from agricultural smudging or industrial operations is excluded in Coverage C—Personal Property.

2-2. The insurer would cover the family's additional living expenses only until July 15, when their home became habitable. Josh would be responsible for the family's additional living expenses after July 15.

2-3. Theft of personal property is not covered under the DP-3, but coverage is provided for damage to covered property caused by burglars, unless the dwelling has been vacant for more than sixty days. Because the house was vacant for only a month, the policy still provides some coverage. The damage to both the door frame and the drawers is covered. Any items of value found in the drawers that were stolen by the thief would not be covered.

Educational Objective 3

3-1.   Owners of mobile homes face loss exposures similar to those faced by owners of conventional homes, including these (any three):

- Damage to or destruction of the mobile home

- Damage to or destruction of other structures on the residence premises

- Damage to or destruction of personal property in the mobile home or in other structures

- Loss of use of the mobile home

- Liability loss because of bodily injury to others or damage to the property of others

3-2.   The construction materials and loose foundation of mobile homes make them vulnerable to additional exposures. Mobile homes are constructed of lighter materials than those used for homes built on permanent foundations, and special construction techniques are used. A mobile home's wheels are generally removed, and the structure is set on blocks, piers, or masonry footings. A mobile home without protective skirting attached to the bottom is vulnerable to a buildup of debris underneath it that may result in damage.

3-3.   The use of mobile homes as vacation homes can affect their vulnerability to additional exposures because they may be located in recreational areas or areas subject to greater loss exposure, such as in the mountains, beside a lake or river, or in heavily wooded areas. The absence of services, such as fire and telephone services, and the absence of nearby neighbors (who could report a fire) can increase the severity if a loss occurs.

3-4.   Certain contents in mobile homes, such as built-in cabinets, appliances, and furniture, are considered part of the mobile home; in conventional homes, such contents may be considered personal property. This distinction determines whether dwelling or personal property coverage applies for such contents.

3-5.   These answers address questions regarding modifications to the HO-3 policy that result from adding a Mobilehome Endorsement and a Declarations page to create a mobilehome policy.

a.   The definition of "residence premises" is changed in the Mobilehome Endorsement to mean the mobile home and other structures located on land owned or leased by the insured where the insured resides at the location shown on the declarations page.

b.   In the Mobilehome Endorsement, Coverage A—Dwelling is changed to apply to a mobile home used primarily as a private residence and the structures and utility tanks attached to it. It also includes floor coverings, appliances, dressers, cabinets, and similar items that are permanently installed. Coverage is provided for materials and supplies for construction, alteration, or repair of the mobile home or other structures on the premises.

c.   The Mobilehome Endorsement adds a unique "property removed" coverage that applies if the mobile home is endangered by an insured peril, requiring removal to avoid damage. This coverage provides up to $500 for reasonable expenses incurred by the policyholder to remove and return the entire mobile home.

d.   The Mobilehome Endorsement provides an additional coverage to repair or replace damaged parts of a series (not the entire series) of panels to match the remainder of the panels as closely as possible or to provide an acceptable decorative effect.

▶▶

3-6. These answers address questions regarding mobilehome endorsements:

    a. The Actual Cash Value Mobilehome endorsement changes the loss settlement terms on the mobile home and other structures (including carpeting and appliances that are included as part of the mobile home under Coverage A) to apply an actual cash value basis rather than a replacement cost basis for losses.

    b. The Transportation/Permission to Move endorsement provides coverage for perils of transportation (collision, upset, stranding, or sinking) and coverage for the mobile home and other structures at the new location anywhere in the United States or Canada for thirty days from the endorsement's effective date. A special deductible applies to this coverage.

    c. The Mobilehome Lienholder's Single Interest endorsement provides coverage only to a lienholder (on request) for collision and upset transportation exposures, subject to numerous recovery conditions. It also provides coverage to the lienholder for any loss resulting from the owner's conversion, embezzlement, or secretion of the mobile home.

    d. The Broadened Residence Premises Definition endorsement indicates a starting date and an ending date within the policy period during which the residency requirement will be temporarily removed. It is used when the insured will not be residing on the premises on the inception date of the policy period.

3-7. These answers address questions regarding the coverage provided in Jake's mobilehome policy/endorsement:

    a. The mobilehome policy/endorsement provides coverage for this residence premises under Coverage A. The Additional Coverage under Section I provides up to $500 for Jake to remove the entire mobile home from the threat of a pending severe storm and return it afterwards. Jake could increase that $500 limit by adding the Property Removed Increased Limit endorsement. The Loss to a Pair or Set Condition in Section I of the Mobilehome Endorsement would cover repair or replacement of any damaged panels on the mobile home to match the remaining panels or provide an acceptable decorative effect.

    b. The Mobilehome Endorsement and the Declarations page in Jake's policy provide all coverages necessary to protect a listed lienholder because the endorsement modifies the word "mortgagee" to include a lienholder. The Transportation/Permission to Move endorsement covers most transportation perils and the Ordinance or Law Coverage endorsement returns coverage for ordinance or law exposures to the policy. The Mobilehome Lienholder's Single Interest endorsement would meet the lienholder's requirement for coverage against secretion and should resolve the lienholder's concerns about transportation perils because it provides coverage only to the lienholder.

Educational Objective 4

4-1. A community's residents become eligible for flood insurance under the NFIP in two ways:

    a. The community applies to the Federal Insurance Administration (FIA) to be included in the NFIP.

    b. The Federal Emergency Management Agency (FEMA) determines that an area is flood-prone and notifies the community that it has one year to decide whether to join the NFIP. A community that chooses not to join the NFIP is not eligible for federal flood assistance.

4-2. If a disaster occurs as a result of flooding in a nonparticipating community, no federal financial assistance can be provided for the permanent repair or reconstruction of insurable buildings in SFHAs. Eligible applicants for disaster assistance may, however, receive forms of disaster assistance that are not related to permanent repair and reconstruction of buildings. If a community is accepted into the NFIP within six months of a disaster, these limitations on federal disaster assistance are lifted.

4-3. When a community first joins the NFIP, property owners in special flood hazard areas can purchase limited amounts of insurance at subsidized rates under the initial phase of the program, called the emergency program. Although the community is eligible under the emergency program, the FIA arranges for a detailed study of the community and its susceptibility to flood. The study results in the publication of a Flood Insurance Rate Map (FIRM) that divides the community into specific zones to identify the probability of flooding in each zone.

4-4. Three federal flood insurance policies are available to insureds:

a. The dwelling form is used for any dwelling having an occupancy of no more than four families, such as single-family homes, townhouses, row houses, and individual condominium units.

b. The general property form is used for all other occupancies—that is, multi-residential and nonresidential, except for residential condominium building associations.

c. Residential condominium building associations are eligible for coverage under the residential condominium building association form.

4-5. The NFIP generally requires a thirty-day waiting period for new flood insurance policies and for endorsements that increase coverage on existing policies. The waiting period prevents adverse selection.

4-6. An exception to the NFIP's waiting period is made for flood insurance that is purchased initially in connection with a new or an increased mortgage on a property. In such cases, the policy becomes effective at the time the mortgage becomes effective, provided that the policy is applied for at or before the transfer of ownership or date of mortgage.

4-7. In the WYO program, the FIA determines rates, coverage limitations, and eligibility. Insurers collect premiums, retain commissions, and use the remainder of the premiums to pay claims. Insurers receive an expense allowance for policies written and claims processed, while the federal government retains responsibility for losses. The NFIP totally reinsures the coverage.

4-8. While the community is in the emergency flood insurance program, only $35,000 in flood insurance is available. If the community complies with the flood control and land-use restrictions required by the NFIP, and the maps are created for the specific flood zones, the community may change to the regular flood program. Under the regular flood program, up to $250,000 coverage is available for dwellings.

Educational Objective 5

5-1. A FAIR plan (or a beachfront and windstorm plan) makes property insurance coverage available when insurers in the voluntary market cannot profitably provide coverage at a rate that is reasonable for policyholders and provide the needed support for credit.

5-2. FAIR plans were created to respond to three types of losses:

- Riot and civil commotion in urban areas
- Windstorm damage to coastal properties
- Brush fires in some wooded, suburban areas

5-3. Whether the FAIR plan operates as a policy-issuing syndicate or contracts with one or more voluntary insurers to act as servicing organizations for a percentage of premiums, the organizations perform underwriting, policyholder service, and claim handling functions. In most FAIR plans, all licensed property insurers are required to share payment for plan losses in proportion to their share of property insurance premiums collected.

5-4. If a property fails to meet the basic safety levels, the owner can be required to make improvements as a condition for obtaining insurance under the FAIR plan. If the problems are not corrected, the state can deny insurance, provided the exposures are not related to the neighborhood location or to hazardous environmental conditions beyond the owner's control.

5-5. FAIR plans usually cover fire, vandalism, riot, and windstorm.

5-6. Some states offer beachfront and windstorm plans that operate using a single servicing organization that provides the underwriting, policyholders services, and claim handling services. Others operate as policy-issuing syndicates in which the plan issues the policies and the plan's staff provides services. In all plans, insurers that write property coverages in that state are required to share in plan losses in proportion to their share of state property insurance premiums.

5-7. Properties eligible for coverage under beachfront and windstorm plans must be ineligible for coverage in the voluntary market and must be located in designated coastal areas. In some states they must be located within a certain distance of the shoreline. Each plan requires that buildings constructed or rebuilt after a specified date conform to an applicable building code.

5-8. The two primary perils insured against under beachfront and windstorm plans are wind and hail.

5-9. Under beachfront and windstorm plans, when a hurricane has formed within a certain distance of the beach area where the property is located, special provisions might restrict applications for new coverage and/or increases in limits.

5-10. These answers address questions regarding Sarah's state FAIR plan:

a. Sarah must have the property inspected by the state FAIR plan administrator. The property must meet FAIR plan inspection criteria, which include basic safety levels, or she must make any recommended improvements to the property before it will be eligible.

b. Because Sarah's state FAIR plan provides coverage against limited perils, Sarah should apply for a difference in conditions policy (DIC) through a specialty insurer. This policy excludes direct loss caused by fire and the other perils covered under the FAIR plan, but it covers the other common homeowners perils.

Direct Your Learning

Other Personal Property and Liability Insurance

Educational Objectives

After learning the content of this assignment, you should be able to:

1. Summarize the coverages provided by personal inland marine policies.

2. Compare the coverages typically provided for watercraft under each of the following:

   - HO-3

   - Personal Auto Policy

   - Small boat policies

   - Boatowners and yacht policies

3. Summarize the coverage provided by the typical personal umbrella policy.

4. Given a case describing a liability claim, determine the following:

   - Whether the loss would be covered by a personal umbrella policy

   - The dollar amount, if any, payable under the umbrella policy

   - The dollar amount, if any, payable under the underlying insurance policies

   - The dollar amount, if any, payable by the insured

Outline

▶ **Inland Marine Floaters**

  A. Characteristics and Components

  B. Common Policy Provisions

  C. Coverages

     1. Personal Articles Standard Loss Settlement Form

     2. Personal Property Form

     3. Personal Effects Form

▶ **Personal Watercraft Insurance**

  A. HO-3 Watercraft Coverage

  B. Personal Auto Policy Watercraft Coverage

  C. Small Boat Policies

  D. Boatowners and Yacht Policies

▶ **Personal Umbrella Liability Insurance**

  A. Purposes of Personal Umbrella Coverage

  B. Personal Umbrella Coverages

     1. Insuring Agreement

     2. Exclusions

     3. Conditions

▶ **Umbrella Coverage Case Study**

  A. Case Facts

  B. Case Analysis Tools

  C. Determination of Coverage

     1. Auto Accident

     2. Slander Lawsuit

  D. Determination of Amounts Payable

Studying before sleeping helps you retain material better than studying before undertaking other tasks.

For each assignment, you should define or describe each of the Key Words and Phrases and answer each of the Review and Application Questions.

Educational Objective 1
Summarize the coverages provided by personal inland marine policies.

Key Words and Phrases

Inland marine insurance

Residence premises

Blanket basis

Inherent vice

Personal effects

Review Questions

1-1. Explain why some insureds might need personal inland marine insurance.

1-2. Identify the general characteristics shared by personal inland marine policies.

1-3. Describe the types of coverage listed in the Conditions section of Insurance Services Office, Inc. (ISO) Common Policy Provisions of a personal inland marine policy.

1-4. How is the amount payable for a covered loss determined according to the Common Policy Conditions applying to scheduled coverage?

1-5. What are the two types of coverage forms available in the ISO personal inland marine program?

1-6. Describe the type of coverage provided by the Personal Property Form of the ISO personal inland marine program.

1-7. Explain why the Personal Effects Form of the ISO personal inland marine program is designed for frequent travelers.

Application Question

1-8. Larry sold his home and most of his furniture. He is spending at least two years traveling by bicycle across the United States and Europe. He is traveling with camera equipment valued at $8,000. He also placed some furniture, books, and personal possessions in a self-storage unit. What personal inland marine policies can Larry purchase to cover his property?

Educational Objective 2

Compare the coverages typically provided for watercraft under each of the following:

- **HO-3**
- **Personal Auto Policy**
- **Small boat policies**
- **Boatowners and yacht policies**

Key Words and Phrases

Perils of the sea

Warranty

Hull insurance

Protection and indemnity (P&I) insurance

Uninsured boaters coverage

United States Longshore and Harbor Workers' Compensation Act (LHWCA)

Review Questions

2-1. Describe the watercraft physical damage coverage provisions listed in Section I—Property of the HO-3.

2-2. What are the watercraft loss exposures covered in Section II—Liability Coverages of the HO-3?

2-3. Identify the types of watercraft coverage available in a Personal Auto Policy (PAP).

2-4. What are the property and liability loss exposures covered under small boat policies?

2-5. Identify and describe the warranties that apply to personal watercraft insurance.

2-6. Identify the entities insured in the boatowners and yacht policy.

2-7. Briefly summarize each of the following coverages typically found in boatowners and yacht insurance policies.

a. Physical damage coverage (hull insurance)

b. Liability coverage (P&I insurance)

c. Medical payments coverage

2-8. Identify the typical exclusions in boatowners and yacht policies that apply to these coverages.

a. Physical damage coverage (hull insurance)

b. Liability coverage (P&I insurance)

Application Question

2-9. Mary insured her motorboat under a boatowners package policy. Explain whether each of the following losses would be covered under Mary's policy. If a loss is not covered, explain why.

a. The front of the boat was badly damaged when the boat collided with a log floating in the water.

b.   The propeller on the boat is rusting and must be replaced.

c.   A small child riding in Mary's boat fell overboard and drowned. Mary was sued by the deceased child's parents.

Educational Objective 3

Summarize the coverage provided by the typical personal umbrella policy.

Review Questions

3-1.   Joe is considering purchasing a personal umbrella policy. Describe who would be covered under this policy.

3-2.   Explain how drop-down coverage applies to a personal umbrella policy.

3-3. Briefly describe the most important conditions in the personal umbrella policy.

Application Question

3-4. Explain whether each of the following losses would be covered by a typical personal umbrella policy.

a. Until the police arrived, the insured detained a youth falsely accused of stealing a racing bike. The police later arrested the actual thief. The youth's parents sued the insured for the false arrest of their son.

b. The insured owns a small bakery and is sued when an employee severely burns his hand when an oven's handle falls off.

Educational Objective 4

Given a case describing a liability claim, determine the following:

- **Whether the loss would be covered by a personal umbrella policy**
- **The dollar amount, if any, payable under the umbrella policy**
- **The dollar amount, if any, payable under the underlying insurance policies**
- **The dollar amount, if any, payable by the insured**

Review Question

4-1. Eileen and Robert are a married couple who own a home and two vehicles for which they are the only drivers. The Insurance Services Office, Inc. (ISO) Homeowners 3—Special Form (HO-3) policy includes liability coverage with a $500,000 per occurrence limit. The vehicles are insured under a personal auto policy (PAP) with split limits of $250,000 per person/ $500,000 per occurrence. The couple also carry a personal umbrella policy with a $1 million limit, a $500,000 deductible (retained limit), and a $1,000 self-insured retention (SIR). All policies list Eileen and Robert as named insureds.

Robert is in an auto accident involving a collision with two other vehicles and is found liable for injuries to the other two drivers. The first claimant was awarded $282,000 for bodily injury, and the second claimant was awarded $325,000 for bodily injury.

a.   What amounts, if any, will be paid under the PAP and under the personal umbrella policy?

b.   Eileen and Robert fail to pay the premium for their auto policy, and the coverage is canceled. Payments were made on the HO-3 and the personal umbrella policies to keep them in force. What amounts would be paid for Robert's auto accident in this instance?

Answers to Assignment 8 Questions

NOTE: These answers are provided to give students a basic understanding of acceptable types of responses. They often are not the only valid answers and are not intended to provide an exhaustive response to the questions.

Educational Objective 1

1-1. Some insureds might need personal inland marine insurance because of the restrictive nature of some personal property coverages under a homeowners policy. Personal inland marine policies can provide higher limits of insurance for losses of a particular type or that occur at a particular location.

1-2. Personal inland marine policies share these general characteristics:

- The coverage is tailored to the specific type of property to be insured, such as jewelry, cameras, or musical instruments.

- The insured may select the appropriate policy limits.

- Policies are often written without a deductible.

- Most policies insure property worldwide with special form coverage (open perils), subject to exclusions.

1-3. The Conditions section of the Common Policy Provisions specifies that insured property may have scheduled coverage by which articles or items are specifically listed. The Conditions section also specifies that insured property may have unscheduled coverage by which articles are covered on a blanket basis, such as stamps or coins in a collection.

1-4. With certain exceptions, the amount paid for a covered loss is the least of four amounts:

- The actual cash value of the insured property at the time of loss or damage

- The amount for which the insured could reasonably be expected to have the property repaired to its condition immediately before loss

- The amount for which the insured could reasonably be expected to replace the property with property substantially identical to the lost or damaged article

- The amount of insurance stated in the policy

1-5. In the ISO personal inland marine program, two types of coverage forms are available:

- Specialized forms are used to cover a single category of personal property, such as outboard motors and boats, fine arts, cameras, or motorized golf carts.

- General forms are broader and generic in nature. These three general forms (Personal Articles Standard Loss Settlement Form, Personal Property Form, and Personal Effects Form) are commonly used to provide coverage on a single form for many kinds of personal property.

1-6. The Personal Property Form provides special form coverage on unscheduled personal property owned or used by the insured and normally kept at the insured's residence. The form also provides worldwide coverage on the same property when it is temporarily away from the residence premises. The Personal Property Form can be used to insure thirteen classes of unscheduled personal property, such as silverware, cameras, and major appliances.

1-7. The Personal Effects Form is designed for frequent travelers because it provides special form coverage on personal property such as luggage, clothes, cameras, and sports equipment normally worn or carried by tourists and travelers. The form covers property worldwide, but only while the property is away from the insured's permanent residence.

1-8. A Personal Effects Form can be used to cover the camera equipment. The Personal Property Form can be used to insure the property in the self-storage unit.

Educational Objective 2

2-1. Section I watercraft physical damage coverage includes these provisions:

- A $1,500 limit applies to watercraft, including trailers, furnishings, and equipment. (For example, an insured's $800 kayak is fully covered for physical damage loss.)

- Coverage is provided on a named-perils-only basis. (The insured's kayak is covered only for the HO-3 Section I perils, not for perils of the sea.)

- Windstorm coverage applies (up to the $1,500 limit) only when the craft is inside a fully enclosed building.

- Theft coverage does not apply to the boat and motor when away from the residence premises; accessories, trailers, and other boating personal property are excluded from this coverage. (For example, the insured's kayak would not be covered if it is stolen from the roof of the insured's car while he or she is traveling.)

2-2. The liability section of the homeowners policy includes a detailed watercraft exclusion focusing on craft of certain size and length. HO-3 Section II watercraft liability coverage, by virtue of the scope of the exclusion, covers only certain limited watercraft loss exposures:

- All watercraft not powered, except sailing vessels twenty-six feet or more in length

- All inboard, inboard-outdrive, and sailing vessels not owned or rented by an insured

- All inboard and inboard-outdrive boats of fifty horsepower or less, rented to an insured

- All sailing vessels with auxiliary power, if less than twenty-six feet long

- All boats powered by an outboard motor or motors, unless the motor both exceeds twenty-five horsepower and was owned by an insured at policy inception

2-3. The PAP provides physical damage loss to a boat trailer if the trailer is described on the PAP Declarations page. Also, a boat trailer the insured owns is covered for liability (regardless of whether it is described on the Declarations page) if it is designed to be pulled by a private passenger auto, pickup, or van.

2-4. Typical property loss exposures covered under a small boat policy could include damage to the boat as a result of a collision with another object, theft of the boat's motor or equipment, lightning damage to the boat's electrical and navigational equipment, and wind damage to a sail.

Generally, a small boat policy includes liability insurance for bodily injury, loss of life, illness, and property damage to third parties arising out of the ownership, maintenance, or use of the boat. Medical payments coverage is typically included for any insured person who sustains bodily injury while in, upon, boarding, or leaving the boat. Liability loss exposures covered under a small boat policy can include bodily injury liability for injuries sustained by passengers when a boat collides with a dock, property damage liability for damage to the dock resulting from the collision, and liability for medical payments to a patron on the dock who sustains a minor leg injury as a result of the collision.

2-5. These are the major personal watercraft insurance warranties:

- Pleasure use—The insured warrants that the boat will be used only for private, pleasure purposes and will not be hired or chartered unless the insurer approves.

- Seaworthiness—The insured warrants that the boat is in a seaworthy condition.

- Lay-up period—The insured warrants that the boat will not be in operation during certain periods, such as during the winter months.

- Navigational limits—These warranties limit the use of the vessel to a certain geographic area (for example, inland waterways and coastal areas only).

2-6. The entities insured in a boatowners and yacht policy include those named on the declarations page, resident relatives of the household, and persons under the age of twenty-one in the insured's care. The insured's paid captain and crew are also considered insureds. Other persons or organizations using the boat without a charge are covered provided the named insured gives permission.

2-7. These answers pertain to boatowners and yacht policies:

a. Boatowners and yacht policies contain physical damage coverage (also called hull insurance) on either a named perils or a special form basis covering the boat or "hull," equipment, accessories, motor, and trailer.

b. Protection and indemnity (P&I) insurance is a broader form of bodily injury and property damage coverage that protects an insured against bodily injury and property damage liability arising from the ownership, maintenance, or use of the boat, and also against crew injuries, wreck removal, and negligence for an unseaworthy vessel. Defense costs arising from any claim, including suits from third parties, are also covered.

c. Medical payments coverage under boatowners and yacht insurance policies includes coverage for such bodily-injury related expenses as medical, surgical, x-ray, dental, ambulance, hospital, professional nursing, and funeral services; and for first aid rendered at the time of the accident.

2-8. These answers address exclusions in boatowners and yacht policies:

    a. Typical exclusions in boatowners and yacht policies apply to physical damage coverage:

- Wear and tear, gradual deterioration, rust, corrosion, mold, wet or dry rot, marring, denting, scratching, inherent vice, latent or physical defect, insects, animal or marine life, weathering, and dampness of atmosphere.

- Mechanical breakdown or faulty manufacturing, unless the loss was caused by fire or explosion.

- Freezing and thawing of ice, unless the insured has taken reasonable care to protect the property.

- Loss that occurs while the boat is used in any official race or speed contest. However, most watercraft policies do not exclude sailboat racing.

- Intentional loss caused by an insured.

- War, nuclear hazard, and radioactive contamination.

    b. Typical exclusions in boatowners and yacht policies apply to liability coverage:

- Intentional injury or illegal activities.

- Renting the watercraft to others or carrying persons or property for a fee without the insurer's permission.

- Liability arising out of water-skiing, parasailing (a sport using a type of parachute to sail through the air while being towed by a powerboat), or other airborne or experimental devices.

- Using watercraft (except sailboats in some policies) in any official race or speed test.

- Losses covered by a workers compensation or similar law.

- Bodily injury or property damage arising out of transportation of the boat on land. (Coverage can be included with the payment of an additional premium.)

- Liability assumed under a contract.

- Injury to an employee if the employee's work involves operation or maintenance of the watercraft (unless otherwise covered by the P&I coverage).

- Business use.

- Discharge or escape of pollutants unless sudden or accidental.

- War, insurrection, rebellion, and nuclear perils.

2-9. These answers address Mary's boatowners package policy:

    a. The hull is covered against damage from a floating log under physical damage coverage.

    b. A rusting propeller is not covered because of the exclusion of general results of direct loss, which excludes loss caused by wear and tear, among others.

    c. The drowning death of a child passenger is covered under liability if Mary is found to be legally liable. Otherwise, the loss is covered under medical payments coverage.

Educational Objective 3

3-1. The policy covers the named insured, resident relatives, and usually persons using (with the insured's permission) cars, motorcycles, recreational vehicles, or watercraft owned by or rented to the named insured. Also, persons younger than twenty-one who are in the care of the named insured or of a resident relative generally are covered.

3-2. The personal umbrella policy typically provides drop-down coverage, which is broader than the underlying coverage. When the underlying insurance does not apply to a particular loss and the loss is not excluded by the umbrella coverage, the umbrella coverage "drops down" to cover the entire loss, less a self-insured retention (SIR). Usually the retention is $250, but it can be as high as $10,000. The SIR applies only when the loss is not covered by an existing underlying policy.

3-3. These are among the most important conditions in the personal umbrella policy:

- The insured must maintain the underlying insurance coverages and limits shown in the declarations. If underlying coverage is not maintained, the policy will pay no more than would have been covered if the underlying insurance was in effect.

- The insured must give the insurer written notice of loss as soon as practicable.

- The umbrella policy is excess over any other insurance, whether collectible or not.

- The policy territory is worldwide.

3-4. These answers address questions regarding a typical personal umbrella policy:

a. Yes. The personal umbrella policy would cover the insured's liability for personal injury, including false arrest.

b. No. The personal umbrella policy would not cover any obligation for which the insured is legally liable under a workers compensation, disability benefits, or similar law.

Educational Objective 4

4-1. These answers address Eileen and Robert's case:

a. The PAP policy will pay $500,000 (the $250,000 per person limit for each claimant). The loss amount exceeds the $500,000 deductible on the personal umbrella policy, so that policy will also apply to this accident. The personal umbrella policy will pay $107,000 (the remaining $32,000 for the first claimant and the remaining $75,000 for the second claimant). Because the loss is covered by an underlying policy, the $1,000 SIR will not apply.

b. If underlying limits are not maintained, the umbrella policy will pay no more than would have been covered if the underlying insurance were in effect. The canceled PAP pays nothing. Because the loss amount exceeds the umbrella deductible, the personal umbrella liability policy will respond. The $500,000 deductible shown on the umbrella declarations page will be applied. The umbrella policy will pay $107,000 for this occurrence. Robert is responsible for the remaining $500,000.

C

Direct Your Learning

Life Insurance Planning

Educational Objectives

After learning the content of this assignment, you should be able to:

1. Describe the financial impact of the premature death personal loss exposure on the following types of family structures:

   - Singles without children

   - Single-parent families

   - Two-income families

   - Traditional families

   - Blended families

   - Sandwiched families

2. Describe the needs approach and the human life value approach for determining the appropriate amount of life insurance.

3. Summarize the various types of life insurance.

4. Summarize the distinguishing characteristics of life insurance provided by each of the following sources: individual life insurance, group life insurance, and government-provided life insurance.

5. Summarize the common life insurance contractual provisions and riders.

6. Given a scenario regarding a particular family structure with its associated financial and family obligations, recommend an appropriate life insurance product, considering the following factors:

   - Need for life insurance

   - Types of life insurance

   - Sources of life insurance

   - Life insurance contractual provisions and riders

Outline

▶ **Premature Death Loss Exposures**
   A. Costs Associated With Premature Death
   B. Singles Without Children
   C. Single-Parent Families
   D. Two-Income Families With Children
   E. Two-Income Families Without Children
   F. "Traditional" Families
   G. Blended Families
   H. "Sandwiched" Families

▶ **Determining the Amount of Life Insurance to Own**
   A. Needs Approach
      1. Final Expenses Needs
      2. Debt Elimination Needs
      3. Family Living Expense Needs
      4. Special Needs
      5. Retirement Income Needs
      6. Life Insurance and Other Assets
   B. Human Life Value Approach

▶ **Types of Life Insurance**
   A. Term Life
   B. Whole Life
   C. Universal Life
   D. Variable Life
   E. Variable Universal Life
   F. Other Types of Life Insurance
      1. Current Assumption Whole Life
      2. Second-to-Die (Survivorship) Life Insurance
      3. First-to-Die (Joint) Life Insurance

▶ **Sources of Life Insurance**
   A.

▶ **Common Life Insurance Contractual Provisions and Riders**
   A. Common Life Insurance Contractual Provisions
      1. Assignment Clause Provision
      2. Beneficiary Designations
      3. Dividend Options
      4. Excluded Risks

      5. Grace Period
      6. Incontestable Clause
      7. Misstatement of Age or Sex
      8. Nonforfeiture Options
      9. Policy Loan Provisions
      10. Reinstatement Clause
      11. Settlement Options
      12. Suicide Clause
   B. Common Life Insurance Riders
      1. Accelerated Death Benefits
      2. Additional Life Insurance Riders

▶ **Life Insurance Case Study**
   A. Needs Analysis Steps
      1. Expense Needs
      2. Special Needs
      3. Retirement Income Needs
      4. Total Needs
      5. Assets Available
      6. Total Life Insurance Needs
   B. Recommendations
      1. Types and Sources of Life Insurance
      2. Life Insurance Contractual Provisions and Riders

study **tips**   **Plan to take one week to complete each assignment in your course.**

▶▶

For each assignment, you should define or describe each of the Key Words and Phrases and answer each of the Review and Application Questions.

Educational Objective 1

Describe the financial impact of the premature death personal loss exposure on the following types of family structures:

- **Singles without children**
- **Single-parent families**
- **Two-income families**
- **Traditional families**
- **Blended families**
- **Sandwiched families**

Review Questions

1-1. Describe the costs associated with premature death.

1-2. Describe the financial impact of the premature death of either spouse in a two-income family with children.

1-3. Describe a "sandwiched" family.

Educational Objective 2

Describe the needs approach and the human life value approach for determining the appropriate amount of life insurance.

Key Words and Phrases

Needs approach

Human life value approach

Review Questions

2-1. Identify the ways an insurance professional using the needs approach would gather facts about a family's financial needs.

2-2. Describe the human life value approach to determining the appropriate amount of life insurance.

2-3.   Explain why the human life value approach typically develops a lower appropriate insurance amount than the needs approach.

Educational Objective 3
Summarize the various types of life insurance.

Key Words and Phrases

Convertible

Whole life insurance

Universal life insurance

Variable life insurance

Variable universal life insurance

Review Questions

3-1. Explain why the duration of term life insurance might appeal to an insured.

3-2. Contrast term and whole life insurance in relation to these characteristics:

a. Premium

b. Risk

c. Duration of financial obligations

3-3. Explain how variable life insurance differs from whole life insurance regarding investments.

Educational Objective 4

Summarize the distinguishing characteristics of life insurance provided by each of the following sources: individual life insurance, group life insurance, and government-provided life insurance.

Key Word or Phrase

Term life insurance

Review Questions

4-1. Explain why individual life insurance is an ideal choice for younger individuals who are in good health.

4-2. Identify the two ways in which group life insurance plans may be financed.

4-3. Identify the factors that determine the cost of an individual life insurance policy.

4-4. Identify the three parties who are eligible to receive Social Security benefits upon an individual's death.

4-5. Identify the most prevalent method for calculating the amount of insurance an individual receives in a group life insurance plan.

Educational Objective 5
Summarize the common life insurance contractual provisions and riders.

Key Words and Phrases

Beneficiary

Grace period

Incontestable clause

Nonforfeiture options

Settlement options

Suicide clause

Rider

Accidental death benefit

Guaranteed insurability rider (guaranteed purchase option)

Review Questions

5-1. Contrast an absolute assignment with a collateral assignment in a life insurance contract.

5-2. Briefly describe five dividend options for a life insurance policy.

5-3. Identify the most common reason why a risk would be specifically excluded under a life insurance policy.

5-4. Explain the purpose of the incontestable clause.

5-5. Describe how a misstatement of sex on a life insurance policy is treated by the insurer.

5-6. Identify the three nonforfeiture options available to life insurance policyholders.

5-7. Identify four life insurance settlement options available to policyholders.

5-8. Explain the purpose of the accidental death benefit rider.

Educational Objective 6

Given a scenario regarding a particular family structure with its associated financial and family obligations, recommend an appropriate life insurance product, considering the following factors:

- **Need for life insurance**
- **Types of life insurance**
- **Sources of life insurance**
- **Life insurance contractual provisions and riders**

Application Question

6-1. Will, age thirty-three, and Erin, age thirty-one, are a newly married couple. Will is an assistant manager at a national electronics chain store and earns $24,000 a year. Erin is a web application developer earning $53,000 annually. They own a condominium valued at $285,000, which has an outstanding mortgage of $231,000. They have two vehicles and $34,000 in car loans, as well as combined outstanding college loans of $126,000. They also have $12,000 in credit card debt, arising mostly from their recent wedding and honeymoon expenses.

Will's employer does not offer any retirement savings plan or other benefits, and, because of his and Erin's current debt, Will is unable to put any savings into a retirement account. Erin has been with the same employer for six years and has been contributing to a 401(k) for five years. Her employer does not provide any matching contributions for the employer-sponsored defined contribution plan. The current value of Erin's 401(k) is $17,000, including investment returns. Erin's employer provides group universal life (GUL) coverage for her in the amount of $50,000. The couple has no personal savings, and any excess money goes to paying down their outstanding debts.

Will and Erin have been considering whether to purchase life insurance, although they are concerned about the costs. They have decided to consult with a local agent to learn more about life insurance products and what their current life insurance needs would be. The agent advises the couple that she will be using the needs approach to evaluate their current financial situation, economic needs, and available resources to meet expenses in the event of their premature death.

The first step in this process is to determine the couple's cash needs in the event of either Will's or Erin's premature death.

Final Expenses Needs

Funeral costs	$ 8,000
Estate settlement	5,000
Federal taxes	0
State taxes	0
Total final expenses	$ 13,000

Debt Elimination Needs

Satisfy outstanding mortgage(s)	$231,000
Eliminate outstanding credit card debt	12,000
Eliminate college loans	126,000
Eliminate outstanding car loan	34,000
Total debt elimination needs	$403,000

Family's Living Expenses Needs

Household maintenance expenses	$ 82,000
Other living expenses	$125,000
Total living expenses needs	$207,000

Total Expense Needs	**$623,000**

Based on a review of the couple's current financial situation, the agent determines total expense needs of $623,000. The agent further decides to include an emergency fund in the amount of $15,000 to cover any unanticipated expenses following the premature death of either Will or Erin. Although the couple is still relatively young and early in their working careers, the agent will also include an amount for future retirement income funding. The calculation for the amount of retirement income would be based on age, Erin's employer-sponsored retirement plan, and available Social Security benefits at retirement age. In this case, the agent will use an amount of $250,000 each for Will and Erin.

The only assets that the couple currently has available are Erin's $50,000 GUL and her $17,000 retirement account, for which Will is listed as the beneficiary. Neither individual would receive survivor's benefits from Social Security until they reach retirement age. Future life insurance reviews may reflect such benefits as the couple's financial and family situation changes over time.

a. Calculate the total life insurance needs for Will.

b. Calculate the total life insurance needs for Erin.

Answers to Assignment 9 Questions

NOTE: These answers are provided to give students a basic understanding of acceptable types of responses. They often are not the only valid answers and are not intended to provide an exhaustive response to the questions.

Educational Objective 1

1-1. The costs associated with premature death are these:

- Lost income—Deceased wage earner's income is lost.

- Final costs—Funeral costs, medical expenses, and so forth.

- Outstanding debts—Credit card debts, mortgage, and so forth.

- Unpaid long-term obligations—To supplement retirement savings and fund college tuitions, child-care expenses, home maintenance expenses, and so forth.

- Estate planning costs—Estate taxes, probate costs, lost charitable contributions, and so forth.

- Unfulfilled family obligations—Both economic and noneconomic; for example, the family's standard of living may be adversely affected, or a child may grieve over the loss of a parent.

1-2. The financial impact of the premature death of either spouse in a two-income family can be devastating when dependent children are involved. The loss of one spouse's earnings can affect the surviving spouse's ability to properly maintain the household, provide for related expenses, fund future retirement, and ensure the financial well-being of the children beyond any governmental benefits they may receive.

1-3. Members of the sandwiched generation include baby boomers, now middle-age, who are providing financial support to both younger and older family members. A typical sandwiched family could consist of an aging parent or dependent family member who receives financial assistance or other types of support from his or her adult child or another younger relative. This same adult child or younger relative, in turn, supports his or her own dependent children; therefore, this is a generation "sandwiched" between an older and a younger generation that both require financial support and care.

Educational Objective 2

2-1. An insurance professional using the needs approach would gather facts about a family's financial needs by asking questions about its economic needs and available resources.

2-2. The human life value approach estimates an individual's income for his or her remaining working life and factors in other items, such as the individual's age in relation to retirement and the cost of self-maintenance. Cost of self-maintenance means that portion of total wages that the wage earner consumes in the course of daily living; the surplus amount is the remaining wages that go to the family to meet its needs. This surplus is the human life value, which would require replacement in the event of the wage earner's death.

2-3. The human life value approach, which focuses on replacing a primary wage earner's lost income, typically develops a lower appropriate insurance amount than does the needs approach, which also considers any unusual expenses (such as the desire to make charitable bequests) and recurring expenses (such as for additional child care required).

Educational Objective 3

3-1. Term life insurance is useful to someone whose current need for life insurance will diminish after a number of years.

3-2. These answers address questions regarding variable and whole life insurance:

    a. The annual premium for whole life insurance is higher than for term life.

    b. The higher cost of whole life insurance could prompt an insured who has limited disposable income to underinsure. This risk is not an issue for insureds with term life insurance.

    c. Unlike term, which provides coverage for a specified period with no cash value, whole life is available to meet financial obligations that continue for a lifetime, such as the expense of a last illness and a funeral.

3-3. A variable life policy is similar to a whole life policy in that it provides cash value over time, but it enables policyholders to choose among investment accounts (mutual funds made up of common stocks, bonds, or other investments) offered by the insurer and to move cash values among these accounts.

Educational Objective 4

4-1. Individual life insurance is an ideal choice for younger individuals who are in good health, as they may find that their positive age- and health-related attributes present premiums that are more attractive than those from other sources of life insurance.

4-2. Group life insurance plans can be financed solely by employers (noncontributory plans) or might require contributions from employees (contributory plans).

4-3. The factors that determine the cost of an individual life insurance policy are the age, gender, health, and habits of the insured.

4-4. The three parties who are eligible to receive Social Security death benefits are an individual's surviving spouse, dependent children, and dependent parents.

4-5. The most prevalent method for calculating the amount of insurance an individual receives in a group life insurance plan is to provide life insurance equal to some multiple of the employee's annual salary, often one, two, or three times rounded to the nearest $1,000. Many insurers stipulate a minimum and maximum amount of insurance that can be issued on any one life within the group.

Educational Objective 5

5-1. An absolute assignment transfers all ownership rights to another party. A collateral assignment is used to assign the policy to another as collateral for a loan.

5-2. Life insurance dividend options include these:

- Cash option—Dividends are paid in cash.

- Accumulated option—Dividends remain with the insurer and accumulate interest.

- Premium reduction option—Dividends can be applied to future premium payments due.

- Paid-up additions—Dividends may be used to buy increments of paid-up whole life insurance.

- One-year term insurance—Dividends may be used to purchase term insurance for one year.

5-3. The most common reason why a risk would be specifically excluded under a life insurance policy is that it involves hazardous occupations or recreational activities of the insured.

5-4. The incontestable clause designates a period, usually two years, after which the insurer cannot deny a claim because of any misrepresentation on the part of the policyowner.

5-5. A misstatement of sex is treated by adjusting the face amount of the policy (when different premiums apply for males and females).

5-6. The three nonforfeiture options available to life insurance policyholders are cash surrender value, reduced paid-up insurance, and extended term insurance.

5-7. Four life insurance settlement options available to policyholders are the interest option, fixed-period option, fixed-amount option, and life income option.

5-8. The purpose of the accidental death benefit rider is to provide an additional death benefit when death results from accidental bodily injury, or accidental means, as defined in the rider.

Educational Objective 6

6-1. These answers relate to the life insurance case of Will and Erin:

a. The calculation for total life insurance needs would be total needs minus total assets. For Will, this would result in a life insurance need of $821,000.

Total Life Insurance Needs	
Expense Needs	$623,000
Special Needs	15,000
Retirement Income Needs	250,000
Total Needs	$888,000
Minus Total Assets	$ 67,000
Life Insurance Needed	$821,000

b. For Erin, the life insurance need would be $821,000.

The agent would most likely recommend Erin, as the higher wage earner, purchase an $800,000 term life policy. The cost of term life at Erin's age would provide a cost-effective solution. Will would also need a term life policy for the same amount of coverage. If the couple could not manage to pay the premium for these amounts, they should consider purchasing as much coverage as they can reasonably afford to meet the surviving spouse's cash needs in the event of the premature death of either spouse. They should review their needs annually and make changes based on their financial situation.

Total Life Insurance Needs

Expense Needs	$623,000
Special Needs	15,000
Retirement Income Needs	250,000
Total Needs	$888,000
Minus Total Assets	$ 67,000
Life Insurance Needed	$821,000

Direct Your Learning

Retirement Planning

Educational Objectives

After learning the content of this assignment, you should be able to:

1. Describe these aspects of retirement:
   - Factors that influence the retirement loss exposure
   - Investing to achieve financial goals
2. Compare the characteristics of traditional IRAs and Roth IRAs.
3. Summarize the following types of tax-deferred retirement plans:
   - 401(k) plan
   - Profit-sharing plan
   - Thrift plan
   - Keogh plan
   - 403(b) plan
   - SIMPLE (Savings Incentive Match Plan for Employees)
   - ESOP (Employee Stock Ownership Plan)
   - SEP (Simplified Employee Pension) plan
4. Describe the following types of employer-sponsored retirement plans:
   - Defined benefit
   - Defined contribution
   - Defined benefit 401(k) plans
5. Summarize the various types of individual annuities.

10

Educational Objectives, continued

6. Describe the following with regard to the United States Social Security program:

   - The basic characteristics of OASDHI

   - Covered occupations

   - The eligibility requirements for insured status

   - The types of benefits provided

▶▶

Outline

▶ **The Retirement Loss Exposure and Achieving Financial Goals**

   A. Factors That Influence the Retirement Loss Exposure

   B. Investing to Achieve Financial Goals

▶ **Individual Retirement Accounts**

▶ **Types of Tax-Deferred Retirement Plans**

   A. 401(k) Plan

   B. Profit-Sharing Plan

   C. Thrift Plan

   D. Keogh Plan

   E. 403(b) Plan

   F. SIMPLE

   G. ESOP

   H. SEP Plan

▶ **Employer-Sponsored Retirement Plans**

   A. Defined Benefit Plans

   B. Defined Contribution Plans

   C. Defined Benefit 401(k) Plans

▶ **Individual Annuities**

   A. Annuity Types Based on the Date Benefits Begin

   B. Annuity Types Based on the Party Bearing the Investment Risk

   C. Annuity Types Based on Premium Payment Method

▶ **Social Security Program (OASDHI)**

   A. Basic Characteristics of OASDHI

   B. Covered Occupations

   C. Eligibility Requirements for Insured Status

   D. Types of Benefits Provided by Social Security

      1. Retirement (Old Age) Benefits

      2. Survivors (Death) Benefits

      3. Disability

      4. Health Insurance (Medicare)

Writing notes as you read your materials will help you remember key pieces of information.

For each assignment, you should define or describe each of the Key Words and Phrases and answer each of the Review and Application Questions.

Educational Objective 1

Describe these aspects of retirement:

- **Factors that influence the retirement loss exposure**
- **Investing to achieve financial goals**

Review Questions

1-1. Identify the objective of retirement planning.

1-2. Identify how individuals can supplement the minimal retirement income Social Security provides.

1-3. Explain the goal of the preservation of capital investment objective.

1-4. Explain the purpose of the investment objective of minimizing taxes.

1-5. Identify four commonly used forms of savings instruments.

1-6. Describe the concept of maturity risk.

1-7. Explain why stocks are the most risky of the commonly used types of investment.

Educational Objective 2
Compare the characteristics of traditional IRAs and Roth IRAs.

Key Words and Phrases
Traditional individual retirement account (IRA)

Roth IRA

Review Questions

2-1. In terms of investor age limitations, contrast traditional individual retirement accounts (IRAs) and Roth IRAs.

2-2. In terms of investment limitations based on the investor's income, contrast traditional IRAs and Roth IRAs.

2-3. Explain how Roth IRAs differ from traditional IRAs when the owner does not start receiving distributions before reaching age seventy-and-one-half.

2-4. Identify the two circumstances under which contributions to a traditional IRA can be deducted from federal income tax.

2-5. Explain why contributions can be withdrawn from a Roth IRA without subjecting the owner to additional federal income tax or penalties, even if the owner has not reached fifty-nine-and-one-half years of age.

Application Question

2-6. Jim, twenty-five, has recently taken a job to support himself as he completes college. Jim's employer does not sponsor a retirement account, but Jim has been able to set aside some of his salary each week for investment in an IRA. Ideally, Jim would prefer not to withdraw any funds from his IRA before he retires, but he would like to deduct the contributions to the IRA from his federal income taxes. Based on this information, should Jim invest the money he has set aside in a traditional IRA or a Roth IRA?

Educational Objective 3

Summarize the following types of tax-deferred retirement plans:

- **401(k) plan**
- **Profit-sharing plan**
- **Thrift plan**
- **Keogh plan**
- **403(b) plan**
- **SIMPLE (Savings Incentive Match Plan for Employees)**
- **ESOP (Employee Stock Ownership Plan)**
- **SEP (Simplified Employee Pension) plan**

Review Questions

3-1. Explain the tax treatment of contributions to a 401(k) and the earnings from those contributions.

3-2. Explain why the amount of savings available upon retirement is unpredictable for an employee participating in a profit-sharing plan.

3-3. Explain why Keogh plans were developed.

3-4. Identify the kind of organization eligible to participate in a 403(b) plan.

3-5. Explain the purpose of the Savings Incentive Match Plan for Employees (SIMPLE).

Educational Objective 4

Describe the following types of employer-sponsored retirement plans:

- **Defined benefit**
- **Defined contribution**
- **Defined benefit 401(k) plans**

Key Words and Phrases

Defined benefit plan

Defined contribution plan

Review Questions

4-1. Describe how an employee can at least partially mitigate the risk that he or she will not receive the full benefit amount promised by the employer in a defined benefit plan.

4-2. Explain why Congress was concerned about the trend of defined contribution plans becoming more common than defined benefit plans.

4-3. Explain what a defined benefit 401(k) plan must have in a defined benefit portion and in a defined contribution portion.

Educational Objective 5
Summarize the various types of individual annuities.

Key Words and Phrases

Annuity

Deferred annuity

Immediate annuity

Review Questions

5-1. Briefly describe the roles of the annuity owner and the insurer that provides the annuity.

5-2. Identify the three general classes into which annuities fall.

5-3. Contrast the manner in which deferred annuities pay benefits and the manner in which immediate annuities pay benefits.

5-4. Identify the primary advantage of a deferred annuity over an immediate annuity.

5-5. Identify the four general categories into which annuities classified by the party that bears the investment risk fall.

5-6. Name which party bears the investment risk in a combination plan annuity.

5-7. Identify the primary difference between a flexible-premium annuity and a single-premium annuity.

Application Question

5-8. What type of annuity would a lottery winner be most likely to purchase to provide tax-deferred safekeeping of the winnings while still receiving periodic payouts throughout his or her lifetime?

Educational Objective 6

Describe the following with regard to the United States Social Security program:

- **The basic characteristics of OASDHI**
- **Covered occupations**
- **The eligibility requirements for insured status**
- **The types of benefits provided**

Review Questions

6-1. Describe what qualifies an individual for "fully insured" status with Social Security, assuming other requirements are met.

6-2. Describe circumstances under which a self-employed individual's occupation is considered a covered occupation under Social Security.

6-3. Name the requirements for an individual to qualify for currently insured status under Social Security.

6-4. State when an individual can receive Social Security retirement (old age) benefits.

6-5. Name two Social Security survivors (death) benefits a surviving wife might qualify for if she cares for an eligible child.

6-6. Describe the purpose of Social Security disability income (SSDI) Monthly Cash Benefits.

6-7. Name the basic benefits that are provided under Social Security health insurance (Medicare).

Answers to Assignment 10 Questions

NOTE: These answers are provided to give students a basic understanding of acceptable types of responses. They often are not the only valid answers and are not intended to provide an exhaustive response to the questions.

Educational Objective 1

1-1. The objective of retirement planning is to accumulate sufficient funds to meet expenses and maintain an acceptable standard of living.

1-2. Individuals can supplement the minimal retirement income Social Security provides with employer-sponsored retirement and pension plans, personal savings and investments, annuities, individual retirement accounts, and cash value from life insurance policies.

1-3. The goal of the preservation of capital investment objective is to maintain the value of investments, rather than increase their value.

1-4. The purpose of the investment objective of minimizing taxes is to obtain a tax savings large enough to offset the lower rate of return, which would result in a higher net rate of return, after taxes.

1-5. Four commonly used forms of savings instruments are savings accounts, certificates of deposit, money market mutual funds, and money market deposit accounts.

1-6. Maturity risk is the risk associated with securities that may mature at a time when interest rates in the capital markets are lower than those provided by the maturing investments, causing the investor to reinvest at a lower rate of interest.

1-7. Stocks are the most risky of the commonly used types of investment because stock prices can go up or down dramatically in a relatively short period.

Educational Objective 2

2-1. In terms of investor age limitations, a traditional IRA restricts eligibility based on the investor's age; a Roth IRA does not.

2-2. In terms of investment limitations based on the investor's income, a Roth IRA limits contributions based on the investor's modified adjusted gross income; a traditional IRA does not.

2-3. Unlike a traditional IRA, Roth IRAs impose no penalty if the owner does not start receiving distributions before reaching age seventy-and-one-half. In fact, during the lifetime of a Roth IRA owner, there are no required distributions.

2-4. Contributions to a traditional IRA can be deducted from federal income tax under two circumstances. First, an individual who is not currently a participant in an employer-sponsored retirement plan can make an IRA contribution that is deductible up to the maximum annual limit. Second, an individual who is a participant in an employer's retirement plan can deduct up to the maximum annual limit for an IRA contribution if his or her modified adjusted gross income is below a certain limit, which, like the Roth IRA's income limitation, is periodically adjusted for inflation.

2-5. Because the contributions, but not earnings, were made with after-tax dollars, they can be withdrawn from the Roth IRA without subjecting the owner to any additional federal income tax or penalty even if the owner has not reached fifty-nine-and-one-half years of age.

2-6. Because Jim does not participate in an employer-sponsored retirement plan, he will be able to make contributions to a traditional IRA and deduct them from his federal income taxes up to the maximum annual limit. Therefore, he should select a traditional IRA.

Educational Objective 3

3-1. Payment of income tax on contributions, and the earnings from those contributions, is deferred until withdrawals are made, which usually occurs during retirement.

3-2. The amount, if any, available to an employee using a profit-sharing plan is unpredictable because employer contributions are discretionary. Therefore, the employee cannot be sure what amounts, if any, will be contributed to the plan in any one year.

3-3. Keogh plans were developed to give owners of unincorporated businesses and other self-employed individuals the same tax advantages when investing for retirement as their employees.

3-4. The kind of organization eligible to participate in a 403(b) plan is a tax-exempt organization that operates solely for charitable, religious, scientific, or educational purposes.

3-5. The purpose of Savings Incentive Match Plan for Employees (SIMPLE) is to encourage employers with 100 or fewer employees to establish qualified retirement plans.

Educational Objective 4

4-1. In a defined benefit plan, the risks that an employee will not receive the full benefit amount promised by the employer can be at least partially mitigated through ancillary benefits, placing contributions in a pension trust, or having terminated plan benefits guaranteed by the Pension Benefit Guaranty Corporation.

4-2. Congress found the trend of defined contribution plans becoming more common than defined benefit plans disturbing because it had created defined contribution plans to supplement, not replace, defined benefit plans.

4-3. A defined benefit 401(k) plan must have a defined benefit portion of 1 percent of an employee's average salary per year of service, up to twenty years. It must also have a defined contribution portion that automatically enrolls employees in a 401(k) plan with a 4 percent contribution unless they decline to participate. The employer must match at least half of the employee's 401(k) contribution, up to 2 percent of the employee's salary.

Educational Objective 5

5-1. The owner of an annuity (who can be an individual or an entity) pays a specified premium to an insurer in exchange for a promise that the insurer will make payments at a specified interval to return the principal, plus interest, to the individual insured (annuitant).

5-2. Annuities can be classified by the starting date of the annuity, the party that determines the investment and bears the investment risks, or the premium payment method.

5-3. With a deferred annuity, benefits are paid at a specified future point. An immediate annuity's benefits are typically paid within thirty days of premium payment.

5-4. The primary advantage of a deferred annuity over an immediate annuity is that a deferred annuity is a more effective instrument for retirement planning.

5-5. The four general categories into which annuities classified by the party that bears the investment risk fall are fixed-dollar annuities, variable annuities, combination plans, and equity indexed annuities.

5-6. In a combination plan annuity, the annuity owner bears the investment risk.

5-7. The primary difference between a flexible-premium annuity and a single-premium annuity is that a flexible-premium annuity enables the annuity owner to decide when to pay periodic premiums, while the owner of a single-premium annuity purchases the annuity using one lump-sum payment.

5-8. A lottery winner would most likely purchase a single-premium annuity to pay a single premium on receipt of the winnings (not flexible-premium) and begin receiving periodic payments soon after purchasing the annuity (not deferred payments).

Educational Objective 6

6-1. An individual qualifies for "fully insured" status by earning forty quarters of coverage. Each quarter of coverage is earned for each quarter of a year that an individual works, so an individual is effectively fully insured after ten full years of work.

6-2. The occupation of a self-employed individual who earns $400 or more in one year and who pays Social Security taxes and earns Social Security benefits is considered a covered occupation.

6-3. To qualify for currently insured status, an individual must have at least six Social Security credits during the full thirteen-quarter period that ends the year he or she dies, most recently becomes entitled to disability benefits, or becomes entitled to retirement insurance benefits.

6-4. An individual can receive retirement (old age) benefits when he or she reaches age sixty-two and has attained fully insured status.

6-5. A surviving wife may qualify for survivors benefits if she is at least age sixty or is disabled and at least age fifty. Additionally, the surviving spouse who cares for an eligible child or grandchild receives a mother's surviving spouse benefit.

6-6. SSDI Monthly Cash Benefits are designed to replace a portion of a wage earner's income for a short period of time if the wage earner becomes disabled because of an injury or illness.

6-7. Medicare provides these benefits: hospital insurance, medical insurance, and prescription drug coverage.

Direct Your Learning

Disability and Health Insurance Planning

Educational Objectives

After learning the content of this assignment, you should be able to:

1. Describe the financial impact of disability and other health-related personal loss exposures on individuals and families.

2. Summarize the distinguishing characteristics of each of the following types of disability income insurance:

   - Individual disability income insurance

   - Group disability income insurance

   - Social Security disability income program

3. Describe the characteristics of the following nongovernment programs for providing healthcare benefits:

   - Traditional health insurance plans

   - Managed-care plans

   - Consumer-directed health plans

4. Describe each of the following government programs for providing healthcare benefits:

   - Original Medicare

   - Medicare Advantage

   - Medicare Supplement Insurance

   - Medicare Part D Prescription Drug Coverage

   - Medicaid

5. Describe the considerations an individual should review when choosing a long-term care insurance policy, including typical benefits provided or excluded, coverage triggers, eligibility provisions, and other economic issues.

Outline

▶ **Disability and Health-Related Personal Loss Exposures**

  A. Disability Loss Exposures

  B. Health-Related Loss Exposures

    1. Long-Term Care Loss Exposures

    2. Insurance Treatment of Disability, Health-Related, and Long-Term Care Loss Exposures

▶ **Disability Income Insurance**

  A. Provisions of a Disability Income Policy

    1. Benefit Periods

    2. Perils Insured Against

    3. Waiting Period

    4. Definition of Disability

    5. Benefits Provided

    6. Renewal or Continuance Provision

  B. Individual Disability Income Insurance

  C. Group Disability Income Insurance

  D. Social Security Disability Income Program

    1. Disability Definition

    2. Monthly Cash Benefits

    3. Establishment of a Disability Period

▶ **Health Insurance Plans**

  A. Traditional Health Insurance Plans

  B. Managed-Care Plans

  C. Consumer-Directed Health Plans

▶ **Government-Provided Health Insurance Plans**

  A. Original Medicare

  B. Medicare Advantage (Part C)

  C. Medicare Supplement Insurance (Medigap)

  D. Medicare Prescription Drug Coverage (Part D)

  E. Medicaid

▶ **Long-Term Care Insurance**

  A. Coverage Basics

  B. Coverage Triggers

  C. Benefits Typically Provided

  D. Benefits Typically Excluded

  E. Inflation Protection

  F. Guaranteed Renewability

G. Nonforfeiture Options

H. Tax Treatment

I. Waiver of Premium

J. Elimination Period

K. Eligibility Provisions

Set aside a specific, realistic amount of time to study every day.

For each assignment, you should define or describe each of the Key Words and Phrases and answer each of the Review and Application Questions.

Educational Objective 1

Describe the financial impact of disability and other health-related personal loss exposures on individuals and families.

Review Questions

1-1. Describe what expenses, other than the costs of living, a primary wage earner who becomes disabled or suffers a serious health condition might incur because of that disability or condition.

1-2. Explain why, even though the majority of Americans are insured under the Social Security disability insurance program, individuals need personal disability insurance.

1-3. Explain how the choice not to purchase health insurance can ultimately cost far more than the insurance premiums that are saved.

1-4. Describe the long-term care loss exposures individuals and families face.

1-5. Name the three sources of both disability insurance and health insurance for individuals who qualify.

Educational Objective 2

Summarize the distinguishing characteristics of each of the following types of disability income insurance:

- **Individual disability income insurance**
- **Group disability income insurance**
- **Social Security disability income program**

Review Questions

2-1. For a disability income policy, explain the difference between a benefit period and a maximum benefit period.

2-2. Explain the purpose of a waiting period in a disability income policy.

2-3. Explain the difference between an "any occupation" definition of disability and an "own occupation" definition.

2-4. Name which of the three types of renewal or continuance provisions offers the insurer the most flexibility. Explain why.

2-5. Describe the benefits to an insured of purchasing individual disability income insurance over group insurance.

2-6. Explain the drawbacks of an employer-provided group disability plan (LTD) compared with individual plans.

2-7. Name two broad protections that are available under the Social Security disability income program.

Educational Objective 3

Describe the characteristics of the following nongovernment programs for providing healthcare benefits:

- **Traditional health insurance plans**
- **Managed-care plans**
- **Consumer-directed health plans**

Key Words and Phrases

Indemnity plan

Basic medical expense coverage

Major medical insurance

Managed care plan

Health maintenance organization (HMO)

Preferred provider organization (PPO)

Point-of-service (POS) plan

Review Questions

3-1. Name the types of insurers that offer traditional health plans to the public.

3-2. Name the most prevalent forms of managed-care plans.

3-3. Explain the operation of consumer-directed health plans (CDHPs).

Application Question

3-4. Brian's employer offers two healthcare plan options: a health maintenance organization (HMO) and a preferred provider organization (PPO). Brian and his wife, Deb, are both recent high school graduates and currently have no known health issues. They would prefer a plan with low premiums and out-of-pocket expenses. The couple are new to the area, and they are not familiar with area physicians or other medical care providers. Which one of the two healthcare plan options would best meet the couple's current needs? Explain your answer.

Educational Objective 4

Describe each of the following government programs for providing healthcare benefits:

- **Original Medicare**
- **Medicare Advantage**
- **Medicare Supplement Insurance**
- **Medicare Part D Prescription Drug Coverage**
- **Medicaid**

Key Words and Phrases

Medicare

Medicare Advantage plans

Coinsurance

Review Questions

4-1. Name the groups of people Medicare covers.

4-2. Explain whether the federal government provides Medicare Part D coverage for all Medicare beneficiaries.

4-3. List the eligibility requirement criteria an applicant must meet to qualify for Medicaid.

Application Question

4-4. Spouses Bridget and Don have both worked in Medicare-covered employment for over fifteen years and are U.S. citizens. At age forty-five, Bridget is diagnosed with cancer and is forced to leave work because of the disability. Don has to reduce his employment to a part-time basis, and, as a result of their reduced income, the couple falls below the poverty level of their state and is left with little discretionary income. Bridget's medical treatments and prescription medicines are costly, and her doctor advises that she will need hospice care within the next four months.

   a. Explain why Bridget would qualify for Medicare and may qualify for Medicaid.

   b. Assuming Bridget did not qualify for Medicaid, explain the likelihood and reasons why these parts of Medicare would or would not meet the couple's needs: Medicare Part A, Medicare Part B, and Medicare Prescription Drug Coverage (Part D).

Educational Objective 5

Describe the considerations an individual should review when choosing a long-term care insurance policy, including typical benefits provided or excluded, coverage triggers, eligibility provisions, and other economic issues.

Key Word or Phrase

Elimination period

Review Questions

5-1.   Describe what long-term care policies generally cover that Medicare excludes.

5-2.   Name typical long-term care daily benefits.

5-3.   Explain the long-term care policy provisions and considerations, in addition to policy benefits, that should be of interest to applicants.

Answers to Assignment 11 Questions

NOTE: These answers are provided to give students a basic understanding of acceptable types of responses. They often are not the only valid answers and are not intended to provide an exhaustive response to the questions.

Educational Objective 1

1-1. The individual would likely incur medical care expenses, possible hospitalization or skilled nursing facility costs, and possible rehabilitation and/or further education expenses to enable him or her to return to work.

1-2. There are limitations to the benefits in the Social Security disability insurance program, so individuals need supplemental personal disability insurance to protect themselves and their families from financial devastation if a disability or an illness should render them unable to work.

1-3. The costs of medical treatments often cause uninsured individuals to avoid treatment for illnesses or injuries until their health has deteriorated enough that more costly medical care is required. An individual who becomes disabled might lose his or her job, along with any healthcare insurance (and disability benefits) provided by the employer. For these reasons, the choice not to purchase health insurance can ultimately cost more than the insurance premiums that are saved.

1-4. Individuals and families can suffer financial difficulties if they experience certain serious medical conditions, such as cancer, dementia, Alzheimer's disease, and multiple sclerosis. Those needing long-term healthcare might require costly skilled nursing care after hospitalization or might need long-term in-home healthcare to assist them with their daily activities.

1-5. Individuals can purchase individual disability insurance or group disability insurance (if available from an employer or association), and they may qualify for government disability insurance. Likewise, individuals can purchase individual health insurance or group health insurance (if available from an employer or association), and they may qualify for government health insurance (such as Medicare).

Educational Objective 2

2-1. A benefit period is defined as the time period for which benefits will be paid to a disabled individual (insured). It ends when the insured returns to work or reaches the maximum benefit period. The maximum benefit period is the longest period for which benefits will be paid to the insured.

2-2. The waiting period offers the insured or group plan provider a mechanism to control insurance costs. The waiting period is the time that elapses after a wage earner becomes disabled and before income benefits will be paid by the insurer. Shorter waiting periods require higher insurance premiums to cover the insurer's costs. Individual insureds often choose the longest waiting period that they can afford.

2-3. An "any occupation" definition means that the individual is totally disabled and unable to perform the duties of any occupation; under this definition, the insurer will not pay benefits if the insured can perform the duties of another occupation or can perform a new occupation. An "own occupation" definition means the insured is unable to return to the duties of his or her specific occupation; under this definition, if the insured is able to earn income from another occupation, but not his or her specific occupation, he or she will still receive 100 percent of the disability benefits.

2-4. A conditionally renewable policy offers the insurer the most flexibility because it provides the insurer with the option to increase the premium and change the policy terms at renewal, and it allows the insurer to cancel the contract if the renewal conditions are not met. The insurer cannot cancel a noncancelable policy, and, provided the insured qualifies for the policy and pays the premiums, the insurer must renew a guaranteed renewable policy.

2-5. Individual disability income insurance is purchased using after-tax dollars, so benefits that are paid are not taxable to the insured and more disability income is available to the insured when it is needed most. Individual insurance does not require membership in a group, and a job change will not affect coverage (as in employer-provided group insurance). Individual insurance does not require tenure before the benefits are available, and limits may be selected to allow the individual insurance to supplement other disability income insurance coverages provided through employers, associations, and the government.

2-6. Because premiums are paid in whole or in part by the employer and because premiums paid by the insured may be deducted from payroll on a before-tax basis, benefits paid to an insured from an employer-provided group LTD are taxed as ordinary income. Because these policies are purchased in bulk, the options are limited compared with those available under individual plans. And under most employer-provided plans, the group disability income coverage ends when employment is terminated. The coverage also ends if the employer fails to pay the premium for the employee or if the group policy is terminated by the employer.

2-7. The Social Security disability income program includes a monthly cash benefit protection for disabled workers and the establishment of a period of disability, which is essential for determination of numerous Social Security benefits.

Educational Objective 3

3-1. Life and health insurers, some property-casualty insurers, and Blue Cross and Blue Shield plans offer traditional health plans to the public.

3-2. The most prevalent forms of managed-care plans are health maintenance organizations (HMOs), preferred provider organizations (PPOs), exclusive provider organizations (EPOs), and point-of-service plans (POSs).

3-3. People covered by consumer-directed health plans (CDHPs) pay lower premiums for their health coverage because the deductibles are high. Using either a health savings account (HSA) or health reimbursement arrangement (HRA), they set aside money that can be used to help satisfy the deductible. HSAs are funded by enrollees themselves, whereas the money in an HRA is contributed by the employer and is not included in the employees' income for tax purposes. Insureds receive deductible-free preventative care.

3-4. A health maintenance organization (HMO) would best meet Brian and Deb's current needs because it would offer lower premiums and low, fixed, prepaid fees with small copayments for routine visits. Because the couple is in good health and is not familiar with area physicians and other medical care providers, they are less likely to want or require the services of out-of-network providers. A PPO plan would be a more costly solution in terms of premiums and copayments but would provide more flexibility for treatment from out-of-network providers, which does not suit the couple's current needs.

Educational Objective 4

4-1.   Medicare covers people age sixty-five or older, under sixty-five with certain disabilities, or of all ages with a disability or end-stage renal disease.

4-2.   Medicare Part D is a voluntary program, and beneficiaries must sign up for Part D. The government subsidizes the costs of beneficiaries' prescription drugs underwritten through private insurance carriers.

4-3.   A Medicaid applicant must meet eligibility requirement criteria including age, pregnancy, disability, blindness, income and resources, and status as a United States citizen or a lawfully admitted immigrant.

4-4.   These answer questions regarding Bridget and Don's case:

   a.   Bridget qualifies for Medicare because she worked in Medicare-covered employment for at least ten years, is a U.S. citizen, and is disabled. State laws would determine whether Bridget qualifies for Medicaid, but her disability, need for hospice care, and low income may provide eligibility.

   b.   Medicare Part A would be provided for Bridget at no cost and would cover many of her medical needs and hospice care. Medicare Part B would cover her additional medical care; however, the cost may prevent the couple from purchasing the coverage. Medicare Prescription Drug Coverage (Part D) would supplement the cost of her prescriptions if it were affordable with their restricted income.

Educational Objective 5

5-1.   Long-term care policies generally cover daily custodial care and long-term nursing care outside a hospital that Medicare does not cover, such as long-term care in nursing homes or custodial care centers for extended periods, skilled nursing care after 100 days, custodial care, nonmedical care that helps an individual with the activities of daily living (ADLs), or intermediate nursing care.

5-2.   Typical long-term care daily benefits are up to $80, $120, or $160, paid over a maximum period of two, three, or four years for the insured's lifetime.

5-3.   Applicants for long-term care policies should consider coverage triggers, inflation protection, guaranteed renewability, nonforfeiture options, tax treatment, waiver of premiums, elimination periods, and eligibility provisions.

Exam Information

About Institutes Exams

Exam questions are based on the Educational Objectives stated in the course guide and textbook. The exam is designed to measure whether you have met those Educational Objectives. The exam does not necessarily test every Educational Objective. It tests over a balanced sample of Educational Objectives.

How to Prepare for Institutes Exams

What can you do to prepare for an Institutes exam? Students who pass Institutes exams do the following:

▶ Use the assigned study materials. Focus your study on the Educational Objectives presented at the beginning of each course guide assignment. Thoroughly read the textbook and any other assigned materials, and then complete the course guide exercises. Choose a study method that best suits your needs; for example, participate in a traditional class, online class, or informal study group; or study on your own. Use The Institutes' SMART Study Aids (if available) for practice and review. If this course has an associated SMART Online Practice Exams product, you will find an access code on the inside back cover of this course guide. This access code allows you to print a full practice exam and to take additional online practice exams that will simulate an actual credentialing exam.

▶ Become familiar with the types of test questions asked on the exam. The practice exam in this course guide or in the SMART Online Practice Exams product will help you understand the different types of questions you will encounter on the exam.

▶ Maximize your test-taking time. Successful students use the sample exam in the course guide or in the SMART Online Practice Exams product to practice pacing themselves. Learning how to manage your time during the exam ensures that you will complete all of the test questions in the time allotted.

Types of Exam Questions

The exam for this course consists of objective questions of several types.

The Correct-Answer Type

In this type of question, the question stem is followed by four responses, one of which is absolutely correct. Select the *correct* answer.

Which one of the following persons evaluates requests for insurance to determine which applicants are accepted and which are rejected?

a. The premium auditor

b. The loss control representative

c. The underwriter

d. The risk manager

The Best-Answer Type

In this type of question, the question stem is followed by four responses, only one of which is best, given the statement made or facts provided in the stem. Select the *best* answer.

Several people within an insurer might be involved in determining whether an applicant for insurance is accepted. Which one of the following positions is primarily responsible for determining whether an applicant for insurance is accepted?

a. The loss control representative

b. The customer service representative

c. The underwriter

d. The premium auditor

The Incomplete-Statement or Sentence-Completion Type

In this type of question, the last part of the question stem consists of a portion of a statement rather than a direct question. Select the phrase that *correctly* or *best* completes the sentence.

Residual market plans designed for individuals who are unable to obtain insurance on their personal property in the voluntary market are called

a. VIN plans.

b. Self-insured retention plans.

c. Premium discount plans.

d. FAIR plans.

"All of the Above" Type

In this type of question, only one of the first three answers could be correct, or all three might be correct, in which case the best answer would be "All of the above." Read all the answers and select the *best* answer.

When a large commercial insured's policy is up for renewal, who is likely to provide input to the renewal decision process?

a. The underwriter

b. The loss control representative

c. The producer

d. All of the above

"All of the following, EXCEPT:" Type

In this type of question, responses include three correct answers and one answer that is incorrect or is clearly the least correct. Select the *incorrect* or *least correct* answer.

All of the following adjust insurance claims, EXCEPT:

a. Insurer claim representatives

b. Premium auditors

c. Producers

d. Independent adjusters